Open **Minded** Torah

Also available from Continuum

Judaism Today, Dan Cohn-Sherbok
Turbulent Times, Keith Kahn-Harris and Ben Gidley

Open Minded Torah

Of Irony, Fundamentalism and Love

William Kolbrener

continuum

Continuum International Publishing Group

The Tower Building	80 Maiden Lane
11 York Road	Suite 704
London SE1 7NX	New York NY 10038

www.continuumbooks.com

British Library Cataloguing-in-Publication Data
A catalogue record for this book is available from the British Library.

ISBN: PB: 978-1-4411-1866-0

Library of Congress Cataloging-in-Publication Data
Kolbrener, William.
  Open minded Torah : of irony, fundamentalism and love / William Kolbrener.
    p. cm.
  ISBN 978-1-4411-1866-0
  1. Religious tolerance–Judaism. 2. Judaism–21st century. 3. Judaism–Relations.
  4. Judaism–Psychology. 5. Judaism–Essence, genius, nature. I. Title.
  BM645.R44K65 2011
  296.09'05–dc22

                                                                    2010042893

Typeset by Newgen Imaging Systems Pvt Ltd, Chennai, India
Printed and bound in the United States of America

For Leslie

לְךָ אָמַר לִבִּי בַּקְּשׁוּ פָנָי אֶת פָּנֶיךָ ה' אֲבַקֵּשׁ
תהלים כז ח

When thou saidst,
Seek ye my face; my heart said unto thee,
Thy face, Lord, will I seek.

Psalms 27.8

Contents

Acknowledgments

Open Minded Torah began with a conversation with Howard Gordon; it took shape with the help of my brother, Michael Kolbrener, and assumes its current form thanks in large part to Yedidya Sinclair. I am grateful for conversations with Zeke Steiner, Robert Daykin, George Prochnik, Jacob Lampart, and especially Jeffrey Perl, Simon Synett, and Shlomo Felberbaum. I owe thanks to Don Mishell and Michal Michelson for their helpful editing, and Daniel Abrams for his patient expertise on editorial matters.

A version of 'Prayer and the People' appeared as a review of *Mishkan T'filah: A Reform Siddur* in *Commentary* (31 December 2007); and parts of 'Open Minded Torah III' appeared in *American Imago* 67.2 (2010): 245–264.

Prologue, Velvel, Govorovo, 1939

'The end is where we start from ...'

– T.S. Eliot, 'Little Gidding,' *Four Quartets*

I am not sure when I found the picture of my great-grandfather Velvel, perhaps on a long Sunday afternoon in a summer in my youth, in the same drawer where I found my father's old tefillin. Back then, in the suburban Jewish Long Island of the seventies, the black boxes of parchments with their leather straps meant almost nothing to me. I gazed at them with the same unknowing indifference with which Velvel seemed to be gazing at me from under the black *kippa*, his face framed by side locks and beard, the brown sepia tones of the photo-graph enlivened only by the clumsy blotches of red above the cheeks bones, the photographer's primitive touch-up.

Had Velvel survived, he might have been Wolfgang in the America of the thirties, Zev in Israel, or William in a later generation. My grand-father, Abraham, left the Polish town Govorovo for New York in 1919 securing, as he was able, exit visas for four of his twelve brothers, before it was too late. Through the twenties and thirties, the letters from Poland came every week to the family in Forest Hills. In the fall of 1939, they stopped. Velvel and his wife Faige Nechama, their seven remaining sons and daughter Devorah, like many of the *landsman* of Govorovo, were probably shot as the Nazis stormed the town after *Yom Kippur* of that year, or murdered after their relocation to the Warsaw ghetto, or Treblinka or Auschwitz. Whatever their fate, on the living room mantel, the picture of Velvel, distant and foreign, is super-seded by one of my grandparents from the twenties, my grandmother, then stylish, a flapper, my grandfather, elegant and entrepreneurial. The holocaust did not so much fade as become willfully exorcised. The Jews of the ghettos and camps of Europe were our demons, by the time of my adolescence, the third generation, they had already been purged.

The photograph went into the drawer with the tefillin. The face of the Jewish past, with my great-grandfather, vanished.

Years later, Velvel reappeared unexpectedly, out of a carton in my aunt's attic from a *Memorial Book* for the town, part of the genre of books written in the sixties by survivors to memorialize the town 'for the younger generation' – though, written almost entirely in Yiddish, the book was not of much use for Americans and Israelis of that generation. In this photograph, Velvel is not posed, not the iconic museum piece, set off in distant past by the airbrush of the photographer. Still devout, he is a *hasid* of *Ger*. He looks younger, with a barely perceptible and knowing smile, eyes – distant but disarmingly familiar – looking up from under a worker's hat. When I brought the book home to Jerusalem, my daughters noted the family resemblance: 'the eyes.' The uncanny, Freud writes, is only familiar because once present, it is now repressed. The Govorovo *Memorial Book* photo reveals a side of Velvel more difficult to relegate to a distant prehistory.

Velvel, one of the 'Well Known Figures and Types' of the Polish town was a jeweler; but the people of Govorovo associated him with the craftsman from the Bible, Betzalel. In Exodus, God says of Betzalel: 'I have filled him with the spirit of God, in wisdom, and in understanding, and in knowledge, and in all manner of workmanship.' And so, the *Memorial Book* recounts, the residents of Govorovo said of Velvel: he was filled with the 'spirit of God' in his craft. When the schoolboys of the town *heder* learned about Betzalel, God's chosen architect to build the sanctuary in the desert, the class *rebbe* did not merely mention Velvel's name, but summoned his image, daunting and tall, beard flowing, eyes sparkling, hands waving; the 'fantastic' presence of Velvel, and Betzalel himself. God commands Betzalel to 'devise cunning works' – King James' translators come close to conveying the Hebrew meaning of the phrase, '*lahshov mahshavot*,' to invest the physical with the divine. So Betzalel is God's master craftsmen, taking 'the spirit of God' and bringing it down to earth through his 'workmanship.' Just as God uses his 'knowledge' to join the letters of the Hebrew alphabet to create the heavens and earth, so Betzalel, the master human artisan, resorts to his 'knowledge' to fuse letters and make worlds. Through conjoining letters, he creates the sanctuary in the desert, enabling God's presence, the *Shekhina*, to dwell in the world.

The human face, the sages say, is connected to the 'knowledge' with which Betzalel links heavens to earth. For the individual man is also a potential vessel for the divine presence, showing in his face. So in Ecclesiastes: 'a man's wisdom makes his face shine.' The 'cunning work' is the 'spirit of God' made physical – whether in the divine presence manifest in the sanctuary in the desert, or the animated face of man, as Velvel's conjured face, showing heaven brought down to earth.

But face in Hebrew – *panim* – is plural, because a face has many aspects. Velvel may have been known as scrupulous in his religious observance, but he showed tolerance to the diverse populace of Govorovo, which was not the homogenous caricature often associated with Europe before the war, but a collection of Zionists, Bundists, Socialists, as well as Amshinov, Volker, and Alexander *Hasidim*. In the *Memorial Book* photo, Velvel is surrounded by his sons, one wearing the grave expression of a scholar, another, the gravity of a business-man, crowned by a fedora. Velvel's forbearance of others emanates from his smile, but especially the recondite eyes peering out from beneath his own modest cap. Like Bezalel, Velvel was pious and worldly, engaged.

The joining of worlds ends for European Jewry, and for Velvel as well, with the *blitzkrieg* of Poland in September of 1939. 'Cunning works' are ideals rendered worldly, but both Velvel and his world were destroyed. This book begins in Govorovo with the trauma that rendered Velvel faceless, but also with a desire, born out of the loss, to emulate Velvel's craft, conjoining letters through a 'knowledge' that begins by re-limning the face, in the process bringing the Torah, also not caricatured or singular, down to earth.

A voice, like the face, *panim* in Hebrew, becomes distinctive through its many aspects. So the essays that make up this collection are not of one voice: sometimes skeptical or critical, they are as often engaged, even enthusiastic. Bringing together Shakespeare and Milton, Einstein and Freud, as well as the sages of the Jewish tradition will likely frustrate those who prefer their religion, or their literature (or whatever) unalloyed. But though the essays in this book are varied, owing as much to hours spent in libraries on the Upper West Side and Oxford as to those spent in Houses of Study in Jerusalem, they aim, as the critic Dr. Johnson wrote of seventeenth-century poetry to discover 'resemblances' in things only 'apparently unlike.'

In aspiring to what Dr. Johnson calls '*discordia concors*' – a paradoxical 'discordant harmony' of perspectives – the essays are most indebted to two contemporary thinkers, the psychoanalysts, Adam Phillips and Jonathan Lear. Though avowedly nonreligious Jews, both show surprising – and unexpected – affinities with the thought of the sages of the Talmud. Phillips, to my mind, echoes the sages who say that when God declares of His work of the sixth day, the creation of man, 'it was very good,' the adverb – 'very' – refers to man. Man is defined by excess, a '*very*-ness,' as it were, beyond category or boundary. So the essays here accommodate excess and express hybridity, what Phillips calls 'voice in the plural.' Lear also acknowledges the presence of 'separate people in the psyche'; but for him, the stress is integrating this heterogeneous population. The ideal of unity also has a source in the sages – that a person should serve God 'with all of one's heart,' with the multiple and sometimes conflicting parts of the soul. Essays on irony, fundamentalism, and love, as well as the manifold other topics of this volume, in sections on 'Self and Desire,' 'Community and Dispute,' and 'Time and Memory,' express difference, but strive, in accordance with Lear's ideal, toward a unity. Central to all of the essays – whether about Talmudic dream interpretation, quantum physics, or a son with Down syndrome – is a receptivity to the voices within, and the belief that only through their expression is a genuine, unforced integration possible.

For those who believe in a strident version of Torah or an 'open-mindedness' that excludes commitment, *Open Minded Torah* may seem like a contradiction in terms. But the volume title comes from the conviction that attuning to the voice from Mount Sinai means first an open-mindedness to the self. For Torah comes down to earth only to one who is proficient in 'knowledge,' the master craft of Betzalel, and that of Velvel as well – a knowledge embodied, and revealed in the human face.

Part I Desire and self

1 Making exceptions

Getting from the house to school in the morning – or rather the two *hederim* that my youngest sons attend – always takes a while. Shmuel, like a seven-year-old version of the English poet, William Wordsworth, stops to marvel at the wonders of nature; while Pinhas, five, comports himself like a young Isaac Newton, pausing to consider how things work. Today, a garbage pick-up fired both of their imaginations. Shmuel seemed to be readying a sonnet; Pinhas an engineering diagram. Yes, getting to school takes a long time.

Between the flights of sublimity and the mechanical inquiries, I pursue another topic, 'How to Cross the Street.' First, an under-undergraduate course in semiotics: 'What do the thick white lines on the pavement mean?' 'What does the blue and white illuminated image of the pedestrian represent?' 'Yes, this is the place to cross the street!'

So we stand and dutifully wait. One car zooms by; and then another. A young father, with an mp3 player – probably listening to a lecture – his five-year-old daughter in tow, crosses down the block, away from the pedestrian crossing. I see Pinhas wondering: 'What exactly is *abba* trying to pass off on us?' 'You don't have to cross here,' he finally affirms, another car whizzing by: 'Look at them.' He points to the father and daughter still in sight and already at the grocery store across the street, poised to buy a white roll and chocolate milk.

I preempt the request I know is coming. 'No, you can't have *lakhma-nia* and *choco*, mommy packed you a lunch.' And: 'Just because other people do the wrong thing does not mean that it's right.' Finally, a car stops, the driver waving us across benevolently. I nod in gratitude – in Israel, traffic regulations are often viewed as suggestions – 'Thank you for abiding by the law.'

Pinhas is first to school today. Shmuel, sometimes shy, is reticent to accompany us, so he waits outside the school gates. A group of boys, pushing their heads through the metal bars, start to tease him, even as I stand by. 'You guys have a problem?' I ask, mimicking what boys typically say when taunting Shmuel, who has Down syndrome. When I come back, Shmuel is still standing there. He looks confused, a departure from his wondrous happy, friendly self: one of the boys is standing with his tongue hanging out with a mocking stare.

When I return home, my wife asks: 'What do you expect?' This was one of the schools that would not take Shmuel: why should we expect more from children than their teachers? Or, a principal who had told us – he has a niece with Down syndrome, so he assured us, 'I know' – that 'mainstreaming is not good for special children.' Besides, he added, 'it would give the school a bad name.'

The Torah enjoins, 'Love your neighbor as yourself,' and in the same chapter of Leviticus, 'You shall love the stranger.' Love the one with whom you identify, as well as the one who seems different from you. Rashi, the eleventh-century commentator who guides generations through difficult passages, writes that the Torah assumes one may come to hate the stranger because he has a 'defect.' His deficiency, whatever it may be, arouses a desire to afflict him, or at least distance him. But the verse continues: 'You yourselves were once strangers in the land of Egypt.' You see him as different, but he is just like you. The stranger's so-called defect, Rashi writes, is your own. That characteristic which we are unable to acknowledge – too painful or unpleasant – we externalize in a hatred for others. We were once ourselves slaves in Egypt, 'strangers in a strange land,' immersed in idolatry. So, we look at the stranger and project upon him that which we fear might be most true about ourselves. But we fear it – this is the Torah's insight – because it is true. We instinctively hate the other for reminding us of the 'defect' which is our own.

The answer to the question opening *Hamlet* – 'Who's there?'– is never simply answered. We have a natural propensity, the Torah tells us, to be in denial about our selves, but also to project onto others the perceived shortcomings from which we most want to escape. We hate the thing which – in a way we cannot yet face – helps to define who we are. Jewish prayer and ritual, as a corrective to those inclinations, refer to the God who took the Jewish people out of Egypt, not the God who created the heavens and the earth, emphasizing: 'Remember who you are, remember from where you came.' Your past – and you – are also exceptional. The verse concludes: 'I am your God' – Rashi explains, both your God and the stranger's. You are not only united in your history; you and the stranger, who you want to distance from the camp, have the same God. So be open-minded to the stranger within.

In the end, we may have more in common with children of difference, like Shmuel, than we are willing to admit. The school principal's protests about mainstreaming may reveal as much about his own personal insecurities – one is not always efficient, brilliant, and scholarly – as about purported concerns for the 'name' of the school. The proximity of children with Down Syndrome, or exceptional children of any kind, make us uneasy about the ways in which we may also be merely ordinary, less than competent, imperfect. How else to explain a school – or a community – that wants to project an image of perfection in order to maintain its good name?

But that image is a communal fantasy, not the Torah's ideal. Keeping special children out of the 'mainstream' may be, in many cases, the right thing. But sometimes, it is as much about parents – or uncles – who nurture images of themselves helping them to forget what they do not want to know. As for myself, I have a lot to learn from the indefatigably questioning and studious Pinhas, but probably even more from my more bashful Shmuel, who takes in the world in awe, and who laughs and dances with unselfconscious glee and abandonment. The stranger we try to flee almost always has an uncannily familiar face. But becoming more tolerant to that which is more singular in ourselves – acknowledging the stranger within – makes it easier to be tolerant of the exceptional in others.

Back on our morning trek to school, walking in the direction of Shmuel's school now, we encounter the bouncy-gait of the nine-year-old Yehuda: 'Good morning Shmuel!' Shortly after, a smiling boy on a bicycle, and an exuberant: 'Shalom Shmuel!' 'He is my friend,' Shmuel boasts loudly. And then the gawky eleven-year-old from down the block, who keeps a rooster in our building courtyard, volunteers, 'Can I walk with Shmuel to *heder*?' We are grateful to the school principal who declared, 'It's a big *mitzva*' to accept Shmuel into the school.

But the children in Shmuel's school, like his brothers and sisters, perhaps benefit most in learning to take for granted – instead of taking exception at – including Shmuel in their play. For from a very early age, children notice the exceptions we make, and turn them into second nature, whether crossing the street in the wrong place or making a new friend, even though he may be a bit different.

2 Do it again, Denzel: Fantasy and second chances

On a recent flight back to Israel from London, I watched part of a mini-film festival on my laptop featuring Denzel Washington – '*my man!*' as he calls Russell Crowe in *American Gangster* – that a friend had prepared. In one of the films – ok, movies – *Déjà Vu*, Denzel works for the Bureau of Alcohol, Tobacco, Firearms and Explosives, and gets to wear one of those cool ATF jackets as he investigates a deadly terrorist explosion on a New Orleans pleasure-ferry.

In the improbable plot, Denzel joins up with a small group of geeky investigators who, equipped with consoles and flat screens and what they claim at first to be cameras, provide unlimited footage from *any* vantage point to any place exactly four days and seven hours prior to their present. In reality, as Denzel figures it out, it is not sophisticated satellite technology and cameras, but a super-advanced machine that allows them to see back into the past, as it was – or is – happening. The team, especially Denzel, focuses attention on a beautiful young woman around whom the ferry-intrigue revolves. All of this is explained by the very Jewish-looking scientist, played by Adam Goldberg, who, in a nod to explaining all of the 'science,' folds a piece of paper in half to demonstrate how time or space fold into each other, allowing for the high-tech voyeurism.

The hokey premise comes off better than it sounds, though, predictably, things go wrong, and Denzel volunteers against Goldberg's protests to go back into the past, though in his underwear (such being the limits of technology), to make things right. Denzel does all this with aplomb. In the end, the ferry does not explode into a million pieces. The girl who dropped her Raggedy-Ann doll into the Mississippi River is not blown to smithereens. And, most important of all, Denzel does get to walk off into the sunset with the dream girl whose autopsy he had attended just days earlier, or, actually, in the weird metaphysics of this film, days *later*.

What is so resonant about *Déjà vu* – especially the ending? The Denzel who investigates the disaster that happened, complaining of lost loves and unspecified personal trauma, goes back into the past, averts disaster, and while dying in the process, leaves the way open for Denzel of the present, the do-over, déjà-vu Denzel. This Denzel – unscathed, innocent – and ignorant of the traumatic future he will not have to live, shows up on the scene to interview the woman who has just seen him die and who, as it happens, is already in love with him. Talk about fantasies.

Déjà Vu elicits the fantasy of second chances, of this time getting it right. The psychoanalyst Christopher Bollas tells of patients, survivors of trauma and abuse, who cultivate relationships – more often codependencies – psychically designed to replicate the relationships that were the source of their original traumas. For Bollas, sadomasochist relationships are the extreme on this continuum of imagined antidotes to the already-experienced trauma. The implicit wish in each of these cases of finding a way of repeating the relationship that caused all of the pain is always the same: 'I will do it again; but this time I will *survive* it.' For the abuse survivor, there is the fantasy that things will be different this time, when in fact, it is always just a repetition: a version of the same.

This is the fantasy that Denzel elicits and fulfills. This time things are different: he really does survive! What makes the film even more affecting is that the 'do-over' Denzel provides just the slightest hint – even though it is impossible within the framework of the story the film tells in which he has never met the girl with whom he drives off – that he *knows* he is doing it again. The movie delivers, with the help of Denzel's knowing smile, the pleasure of getting to do it over, but this time get it right. So, the life that had been characterized by loss, the errors and mistakes that could have been avoided are, in this fantasy, averted.

'Jealousy,' the sages say, is one of the things that take a person 'out of the world.' We may acknowledge that we are jealous of others, but are not as likely to admit that sometimes we live as if we are jealous of ourselves, of the person we might have been if only we had acted differently. If we had gone to a different school, or taken a different job, or moved to a different city, or just said a different – this time the right – thing. When choices made, in retrospect wrong ones, linger in our minds as irrevocable catastrophes, as life-changing events that leave us without hope, then we are most susceptible to the jealousy that keeps us living in the past. Jealous of the person we might have been – the person who emerges unscathed and smiling – we make ourselves vulnerable to repetition, to the stagnation and lamentation over what we were not able to become. This is the jealousy where we remain in fantasy, the fantasy of the 'if only.' Sometimes our friends or relatives encourage these stagnating fantasies, goading us in the belief that other choices would have served us better, making us abandon the present in which we live.

In the movies, trauma is averted, '*déjà-vu* Denzel' shows up at the site of an averted catastrophe, and falls in love again with the woman whom he has already loved and lost. This Denzel avoids loss. If only. In real life, not the movies, the challenge is to acknowledge loss, and a life chosen, but always still in-the-making. Instead of pursuing the repetitions, of which the jealousy of the hypothetical selves we might have been is the symptom, we inhabit the present, and acknowledge missed opportunities, but also exhibit courage and creativity in the face of loss. For the jealousy of what I might have been – the Hollywood fantasy of my hypothetical self – takes me out of my world, thus leading me to forget that the choice of my present is always for the first time.

3 Caught in the act: Torah and desire

'*A person is known for three things: his cup, his pocket, and his anger*, and some say, his play.'

– Talmud

My wife was away. The usual escape route to my office – the quiet place to prepare for a class on Sidney's *Defense of Poetry* – was blocked. So I sat at the dining room table, trying to concentrate. But with three of my girls – nine, twelve, and fourteen – dancing to 'Jewish' disco, and the two youngest busy dismantling the house, getting through Sidney was impossible. The girls were cute, retracing the intricate steps they had learned in their ballet class. But, my gaze upon them, I noticed their romping dance suddenly transform into a performance. Freidie extended her leg with the slightest extra touch of affected grace, and Chana's plié became more self-conscious, artful. I had caught them in the act.

In the 1930s, the psychoanalyst Marion Milner encouraged her patients to doodle as a kind of therapeutic scribbling. But some were unable to bear the 'chaos and uncertainty' of something unfinished. They hurried to turn their doodles into pictures that would be recognizable and whole. The children's thoughts and moods may have been developing, Milner notes, but their pictures, already finished images, preempted them. Children who 'catch themselves in the act' show a need for a 'false certainty' as they give up the freedom of their play for something final and fixed, prematurely achieved.

Teachers, cultures and parents sometimes discourage the uncertainty of play, preferring an education based upon 'compliance' – to external standards and norms – that leads, as Adam Phillips writes, to becoming 'like somebody who knows certain things.' Becoming proficient may mark the beginning of education, but absent, in the education based upon compliance, is the self who comes into being through play.

Play – before the premature 'finish' of the overly artful dance or the forced smiles of the school snapshots – creates new possibilities. The poet, T.S. Eliot writes, is 'constantly amalgamating disparate experiences.' The ordinary man 'falls in love, or reads Spinoza, and these two experiences have nothing to do with each other, or with the noise of the typewriter or the smell of cooking.' But for the poet, the cerebral 'reading Spinoza' and the sensual 'smell of cooking' come together to form new wholes. For Christopher Bollas, the self finds her voice – what he calls, playing on the Freudian term, a 'personal id-iom' – through a 'play that allows for the possibility of new connections.' Through engaging with the outer world, she generates her self. But the ability to tolerate not knowing – not having a finished form – is an important part of the receptive process of play. This is true, Bollas writes, not only for poets, but for scientists and mathematicians as well. Einstein talks of 'combinatory play' as the 'essential feature in productive thought,' a play allowing for new connections and relations. For the mathematician Henri Poincare, the finality of the scientific theory comes only after not knowing – 'I was ignorant.' Bollas sees the self at play, whether poet or scientist, acting out what he class calls the '*eros* of form,' with the id-iom expressing itself from inside out, not imposed from the outside.

King David knows the power of external form, the divine name, but also the energies within. In the midrash, or interpretive story the sages tell filling in the gaps of scripture, David, at the founding of the Temple in Jerusalem, finds the energies of the 'deep' struggling to express themselves. 'When David began to dig the foundations of the Temple in Jerusalem, he dug fifteen cubits, but still did not reach the depths of the earth. Finally he found a shard and tried to lift it.' But the shard talks back: 'do not lift me because I am holding back the deep.' To which David asks: 'how long have you been here?' The shard responds, 'since God proclaimed on Mount Sinai, "I am the Lord your God."' But 'David does not listen, and he lifts the shard, whereupon the waters of the deep rose up to inundate the world.' David knows the forces of the depths, and the power of the divine utterance to hold them down. Yet, he does not listen, for David wants access to the deep.

The sages give another account of the Temple's founding where David himself writes the divine name on a shard to restrain the waters from flooding the world. But when David sees that placing the divine name on 'the deep' causes the waters to recede sixteen thousand cubits, he composes the fifteen 'psalms of ascent.' As the waters ascend, a thousand cubits for each psalm eventually settling a thousand cubits below the earth, David says 'the closer the waters are, the more they will water the earth.' The divine name restrains the waters, but too far back. Uncontrolled, they will destroy the earth, though without those waters and their energies, the world cannot be sustained. The 'deep' cannot be allowed to go unchecked, but it also cannot be pushed too far away. The forces therein were also created by God. The law – the shard with the divine name – is necessary, but so are the forces of the deep.

The cosmic principle is also a psychic one: the forces of the deep are present in man as part of his creation. A philosopher, in conversation with Rabban Gamliel, took matters differently: 'Your God is a great artist, but he had raw materials at his disposal.' The philosopher provides a list: 'Chaos and the void, the deep, the wind, water and darkness.' The philosopher, an Aristotelian, contends that God benefitted from raw materials *not* of His creation. Rabban Gamliel turns on the philosopher with the curse: 'May your soul be blasted,' then, citing verses from the Torah showing how all of the 'raw materials' are creations of God: 'I form the light and create darkness,' from Isaiah; 'He forms the mountains and creates the wind,' from Amos. Not only light, darkness, and the wind, but all of the forces of nature – as Rabban Gamliel demonstrates through chapter and verse – are of divine origin. The philosopher is cursed, and his 'spirit is blasted' because he does not recognize that his 'spirit' or *ruach* – the same word in Hebrew for the 'wind' of the verse from Amos – is a divine creation. Cursed is the man, says Rabban Gamliel, who does not acknowledge that the spirit which he feels within him, sometimes as if swelling from the depths, was placed there by the Creator. These are the forces of the deep, present in the self as well. Though sometimes they need to be restrained, one who disavows or represses them is 'cursed.' The same forces David cultivates in the cosmos in founding the Temple are present in the self. To develop as a self, the deep must express itself and not be prematurely constrained with an external form, a name.

Rabban Gamliel's philosophical counterpart may think otherwise, but the desiring self, the self filled with 'spirit', and the knowing self, are the same. To the question, 'Who is wise?' Ben Zoma answers: 'He who learns from all men.' The measure of the wise person is not the books in his personal library or his collection of Torah databases, but a readiness to learn. That readiness is not calculated by an external measure, but by desire that comes from the depths. He yearns – we see his visceral longing in his willingness to learn from everyone – for knowledge. One earns the title of *hakham* or a wise man, not, says the Maharal of Prague, because of the 'house in which one lives'. Not the building, the name or the external form bestows status, but the identity of the wise man emanates from the depths of the desiring soul.

Learning from only one teacher, even the most preeminent rabbi in town, may show cachet and the need for affiliation, but not a longing to know. The frenetic quest for affiliation is a symptom of learning as 'compliance' that may fend off the part of the self that wants to be other than 'someone who looks like he knows something'. Some choose to perform the part of wisdom rather than be wise. But performing wisdom is a sign of its abandonment. For the Maharal, following Ben Zoma, the wise person is not one who acquires knowledge, topping up his intellectual bank account, but one who shows himself willing to receive from all people, of whatever stature. This openness to wisdom is not just passive, a receptive desire, but an active yearning of one who strives to know. Striving entails the willingness to not know – to even fail – as the sages say, 'a person cannot stand in Torah unless he first stumbles.' Those who perform their wisdom – and there are many in this generation with no forbearance for stumbling of any description, neither from themselves, nor from others – have closed off the energies within.

The wise man is always in the midst; he never fully knows. For a later sage of the Talmud, Rabbi Yosi, what underlies Ben Zoma's conception of wisdom becomes a principle of action and service: 'Let my portion be with those who die on the way to a *mitzva*.' Rabbi Yosi, in placing his lot with those who die in the midst of their performance of God's will, does not contemplate an early demise. But those 'on the way,' with whom Rabbi Yosi wants to be counted, are unencumbered by reflections about the status that comes through completion of an act. The world we live in, to the sages, is 'better' than 'the world to come' because it a place of action – good deeds and dynamic striving. The 'world to come provides' unimaginable pleasures, but its satisfactions are those of repose, the soul at rest. In this world, one who has already done the *mitzva*, unresponsive to further demands, is no longer striving, 'on the way'; though he has earned a reward, even gained a name, he is inferior to one who is in the midst.

So the next time the girls dance while I am in the room, I will try to stick to my reading. Maybe once or twice, I will sneak a look, careful not to catch them in the act, because, more than anything, I want them to keep on playing.

4 Just dreamin': The Talmud and the interpretation of dreams

I had a dream last night. Not a nightmare, but I woke up feeling dread. I have had dreams like this before about which I may remember only a particular image – a set of broken swords lying on a snow bank; a 'boom box' perched precariously on a high shelf, defying gravity; a motor-scooter, luminous green, parked on the wrong side of the street. None suggest danger or are even menacing, yet I wake up from them feeling they might mean something terrible and important that I very much want – or is it that I do not want? – to know.

The sages say that a dream is one-sixtieth part prophesy; after all, God speaks to the prophets through dreams. The other parts of dreams, the sages say, come from 'the innermost thoughts of the heart.' We know where dreams come from, yet we repress them, or we feel dread on their account, or maybe we repress them because we feel dread. The possibility of their significance is overwhelming, so we move on. My eight-year-old recounted her dream when she woke up; by the afternoon, when I suggested we talk about it again, she had already forgotten: 'What dream?' Repression is not a skill that needs practice or training. But Rav Hisda says, 'A dream that has not been interpreted is like a letter that has not been read.' The message comes, and has my name on it. But I prefer to put it under the pile, or like the urgent e-mail that I want to avoid – one click, and delete.

Rav Hisda insists, 'Open the letter, read it.' The Talmudic principle of dream-interpretation may make it more likely for me to heed Rav Hisda and confront the message in my dreams: 'Dreams go according to the mouth.' Perhaps this is the place to suggest the sages were 'postmodernist' before their time, believing that everything is a matter of how I look upon it – 'It is all subjective' – entirely dependent on interpretation. But the same rabbis affirm that a dream needs to be 'interpreted according to its content.' For Joseph in Pharaoh's palace, the Torah says, interpreted the dreams of the wine steward and the butler, 'each according to *his* dream.' Dreams may go after the mouth, but the dreamer must be faithful to the dream dreamt. The interpretation of a dream is constrained by its content; I have to give an explanation of what is there.

Dreams provide an opening into parts of the soul which have not yet been fully acknowledged, and which in conscious everyday life are not fully known. 'Open the letter!' may not be far distant from the Socratic demand to 'know thyself', for interpreting a dream opens up communication within the soul, allowing for self-knowledge. The analyst is always making introductions, writes Adam Phillips, between different parts of the psyche. So dreams are invitations to meet those parts of the soul with which we have not yet made formal acquaintance. Dream interpretation allows the 'innermost thoughts of the heart', the letter opened, to come into conscious life.

But the innermost thoughts are varied. Rav Bana'a had a dream, and each of the twenty-four interpreters to whom he went, provided a different interpretation. Later, Rav Bana'a says, 'all of them were fulfilled' – they all came to pass – because all the twenty-four meanings were latent within it. A good interpretation is one that through speech – because dreams 'go according to the mouth' – brings one or more of those inner thoughts of the heart into consciousness. The 'validation of a good interpretation is internal', Jonathan Lear writes; so dream interpretation is a means of integrating the self. A good interpretation makes sense to me, as I give a voice to that which had never before been heard. Jungian archetypal images and dream dictionaries are of no interest, because they are external to the one who dreams. So the dream interpreters in the Egyptian court, the wise men and magicians, could not interpret the dreams 'for Pharaoh.' Pharaoh's magicians provided interpretations – they may even have been excellent and ingenious – but they were not resonant *for* Pharaoh. Only interpretations that are accepted by the heart of the one who dreams are 'true.' The question the rabbis ask: What does the dream mean to me?

There is a good reason for the insistence: 'Open the letter' – the stranger within may not bear a message I want to hear. But without reading the letter, I remain in silent battle with that part of myself I do not confront, instead of acknowledging it as a part of who I am. This is not just a question of recognizing unpleasant truths or desires, but of expressing them, interpreting them, and in so doing, as Lear suggests, raising them to a higher level. In this sense my dreams are prophetic: my soul bears a secret, but only through my interpretation of the secret do I realize its prophetic message.

The one who sees a river in a dream, Rabbi Yehoshua ben Levi says, should get up in the morning early and recite the verse from Isaiah, 'Behold I will extend peace to her like a river' before another verse from Isaiah comes to his mind, 'the enemy shall come like a violent river.' The dream – the inner world – portends both peace and violence. Since the dream goes 'according to the mouth,' the sage advises: say the first verse from the prophet to bring out the part of the soul that tends towards peace. Not a magical incantation, but a way to activate the inner voice that portends peace. Interpreting a dream in this state of mind enacts an integration of the soul, leading toward a future of peace.

There is no escaping the dream, or the unconscious, or the stranger within. When on the Jewish holidays, the *kohanim*, or priests, stand with their backs towards the ark chanting their blessing, some congregations intone their own supplication – about dreams. We do not ask that bad dreams be nullified; you cannot eradicate the stranger within. He will not go away, nor will the dreams. So we ask rather that the ambiguous dream, one laden with dread, undergo transformation: 'And just as You transformed the curse of the wicked Bilaam' – the Midianite prophet in the Book of Numbers who tried to curse the people of Israel – 'so may You transform all of my dreams for the good.' Bilaam's curse was transformed, through God's love, into a blessing, so we ask, through recognizing our inner voice, and treating it with love, that dreams be changed for the good.

The sages provide further instruction for this 'dream prayer.' The congregation should end their supplication as the priests finish the blessing that ends with '*shalom*' or 'peace.' One who finishes before the priests are to intone: 'You are Peace and Your name is Peace; may it be Your will that You grant us peace!' But before peace between the warring parts of the psyche can be achieved, Rav Hisda's advice has to be followed: open the letter of the dream. One who has an ambiguous or threatening dream, the sages advise, should assemble three friends, and have them recite three verses of 'transformation' from the Torah, then three verses of 'redemption', and finally three verses of 'peace'. Transforming the dream first leads to redemption, and then finally to the end of all Jewish prayer, peace. Not the peace between men, but what always comes first for the sages, the internal peace of the integrated soul.

5 The big game: Baseball, John Milton, and making choices

'What is it with you and baseball?' my wife asked recently after I emerged late for breakfast from my basement office. 'It's a Jewish sport,' I told her. Not because there may be a disproportionate number of baseball players in that classic volume, *Jews in Sport*. There is rather something about the sensibility of the game that makes for the connection between baseball and the Jews.

'And the Mets won last night,' I added. Unimpressed, and unwilling to indulge me further: 'Are you having oatmeal this morning?' But after *shul* – morning prayers – and before getting ready for work, I had heard the results on internet radio, the Mets station, WFAN. It was a big win, the second straight and their sixth of the last nine, and it happened in dramatic fashion. The Mets were down twice, and came back each time. In the second instance, the Mets tied the game in the ninth with a pinch-hit homerun, and though they threatened to lose by giving up a run in the top of the twelfth [extra innings for non-American readers], a rookie and new name on the Mets roster singled in the tying and winning runs. I heard all of this during an update which segued into a call-in program for fans (people up at 1:30 a.m. in the morning and me) wanting to discuss the latest exploits of the Amazin' Mets. I was tempted to call, but embarrassed at the prospect of introducing myself as 'Bill from Jerusalem.' There were other callers; one enthused, 'The Mets are back! It's great to be on top again.'

'Back on top again'? It was only June, and baseball, with 162 games over six months, is a very long season. As the political commentator George Will once deftly offered, 'You can't grit your teeth through the baseball season.' It is simply too long for the investment of emotions in a single moment. Teeth-gritting is for other sports, football perhaps, but certainly not the summer game. There is a rhythm to the long baseball season, and one game, however exciting and seemingly momentous, does not a beat make. Baseball, rather, is a game of stories, complicated, intertwining, entangled which is one of the things that makes for the special connection between baseball and the Jews. Bartlett Giamatti, the former commissioner of baseball and comparative literature professor, likened the game to Homeric stories of homecoming: but before the Greek *ba'al teshuva* (literally the one who returns) Odysseus left his hometown, Ithaka, Jews have been telling stories, making baseball the Jewish sport.

Recently, an older friend of mine, a fan of the Atlanta Braves – for the uninitiated, the Braves are one of the Mets' arch rivals – mentioned in passing, at the end of an email, that the Braves had taken the first two of four games against the Mets. Though he was enjoying the moment, he did not gloat (they ended up splitting the series); his enthusiasm for the recent Braves' victories was qualified by thoughts for what he called 'the long summer ahead.' This showed the attitude of the mature baseball fan, at once immersed in the moment, but at the same time conscious of the bigger story.

One can have the typical baseball fan's attitude about time and story-telling, or cultivate the perspective of my friend. To the typical fan – 'John from the Bronx' in the middle of the night on WFAN – individual moments are invested with momentous importance of great triumph or catastrophic defeat. A good job interview, a promotion, a compliment received becomes a positive referendum on the self, the opposite a disastrous affirmation of failure. Acceding to such referenda on the self may not seem so unwise, except when they go bad: the job interview didn't go as well as you had thought; your coworker was promoted to an even better job; the compliment was followed by a verbal twist of the knife. We can be nourished by the moment, gaining strength from successes, even if only temporary and apparent, and learn lessons from failures as well. But when they become more than that – definitive snapshots of ourselves placed on our psychic mantles – we are guilty of misusing the moment. In the days of social media, we engage in obsessive quests for those mini referenda on the self – the count of followers on twitter and facebook friends.

But obsessing in this way is a sure sign that we are not aware – or are avoiding – the demands of the larger story.

For the baseball fan, to view a temporary success as defining – 'It's great to be on top again' – or the converse – 'It's all over now'– shows a failure to see the whole season, and, in the larger picture, to see how our lives and stories are not always subject to our control. Investing a particular moment or choice with ultimate significance is a kind of contemporary idolatry, a belief in the power of the self or money or your boss, or whatever you may happen to believe is the determining factor of your life. Acknowledging that there are other variables, maybe even an infinite number, is the first step to recognizing the divine, and the role of (what sometimes get simplified) as providence. Milton got it right when, in *Paradise Lost*, he calls Adam and Eve 'authors to themselves,' but also refers to God as the 'Author of all Things.' The philosophers might object to Milton's contradiction, but the paradox tries to make sense of a world in which the creative self and a knowing God coexist. We live in the moment, and narrate the story or various strands of the different stories that make up our lives. But that story is dependent upon another story – which we do not always fully know – that composed by the 'Author of All Things.' To recognize our place in that larger story is to move past the sensibility expressed in the contemporary mantra, 'people make choices.' To be sure, we do make choices, but those choices do not always lead to results we anticipate.

So as baseball fans, we may relish the moment – 'The Mets win!' – but also understand that it is just a passing moment in time, part of a whole season. As Jews we realize that we make choices and live in the moment with all of the intensity which it demands, while never losing sight of the larger frame, how our own stories fit into the larger and precedent stories of which there is only one sole Author. So the 'big game' may offer thrills of victory or agonies of defeat, but we have to remember that, in the end, it is a long season.

6 Of rabbis and rotting meat

We moved to Roslyn on the North Shore of Long Island when I was three. Years later, I was invited to the party of a friend who had moved out of the neighborhood to somewhere on the South Shore. A few of the children, surprisingly, wore *kippas*, and the parents of my friend, perhaps newly religious, bought a real kosher cake. Those were the days before fancy icy decorations meant making an appointment with a 'confectionary artist' in a Greenwich Village loft. True, one of the cars of the blue-frosted train looked like a flower with wheels, but it did not matter to me, or from the looks of it, any of the other children. When it came to the birthday boy to divide the cake, no suitable kosher knife was found. Upon realizing this dilemma, one of the fathers ran from the house, presumably to his car, to retrieve a screwdriver; on his return, he attacked the cake, cutting inelegant jagged pieces. The rest of the parents, unimpressed by the intervention, were silent, the 'birthday boy' stunned. That was probably the last time anyone in his family arranged for a kosher meal.

Our sages ask: 'From where do we know that a *talmid hakham*, a Torah scholar, without *da'at* – the word loosely translated as 'knowledge' – 'is worse than *neveila*, rotting meat left on the slaughterhouse floor for the dogs?' They answer by citing the opening verse in Leviticus: 'And the Lord called unto Moses, and spoke to him out of the tabernacle of the congregation.' The sages explain: 'Moses, the father of wisdom, the father of prophesy, who enacted God's will in performing His miracles, in taking the people of Israel from Egypt, in splitting the sea, in ascending to Sinai to bring down the Torah, in working to build the sanctuary, that very Moses waited to enter the tent of the meeting until he was called: "And the Lord called unto Moses ..."' Of all of Moses' attributes, the one singled out by the sages, more than the miracles performed through his hand, is his sense of timing. Moses did not show up and declare, 'God, I am here,' but waited to be called. Moses was sensitive to the demands of the moment. Moses had 'knowledge' or '*da'at*.'

Someone can be gifted, even brilliant, and sit in the House of Study for many years. But if he does not have *da'at*, he is worse than that piece of rotting meat. *Da'at* is one of the words of which Freud writes in his essay, 'The Antithetical Meaning of Primal Words,' that not only has different connotations, but opposing meanings. Betzalel joins worlds through the very same kind of knowledge, constructing the sanctuary in the wilderness, bringing upper and lower worlds together. *Da'at* is a way to make connections, as in the verse from Genesis, 'And Adam knew Eve.' But the sages also associate this kind of knowledge with the capacity to distinguish and separate; *da'at* for the Maharal is the intellectual faculty to distinguish between opposites. So the primal intimacy between Adam and Eve requires both aspects of *da'at*: before Adam 'knows' Eve, he first recognizes her as separate. Joining requires the capacity to see differences; connectedness requires understanding that the world is more than just an extension of the self.

The power of *da'at* – union achieved through recognizing difference – is not, however, only shown in relation to the outside world: a *bar da'at*, a person with this kind of knowledge, distinguishes and connects the different parts of his internal world. Francis Bacon writes that there are two kinds of people in the world, those who make distinctions and those who find similarities. The *bar da'at* is both. He first makes distinctions: there are some demands of the internal world he will not heed. Metaphors abound to describe the part of the self producing desires to which a *bar da'at* must say 'no': the sages call it the *yetzer ha-ra*, or evil inclination. But even here '*da'at*' contains its opposite. The prophet says, 'On that day you shall *know*' – *ve-yadata* – and 'place it on your heart that God is one in the heavens above and the earth below.' God's unity is affirmed in the heavens, and then on earth: through *da'at*, the abstract ideal rests on the heart, in this world. *Da'at* – knowledge of the heart – is an act of internalization, bringing the knowledge of Torah down to earth. The *bar mitzva* boy wears *tefillin* on his head and arm to show the unity of thought and action; on the day of his *bar mitzva*, he becomes a *bar da'at*.

One who has *da'at* always waits for the call of the moment, and asks himself: 'What does this situation demand?' In heeding this question, he shows that Torah makes a difference in what he does. Like Betzalel, he joins heaven and earth. 'Just as every face is distinctive,' the sages say, 'so every *da'at* is different.' What makes a person distinctive is the way he brings his portion in Torah – what he has learned from parents, community and teachers – into the face which he shows to the world. Torah is not abstract knowledge, but embodied and lived, revealed in his countenance.

So the *talmid hakham* without *da'at* is worse than rotting meat. *Neveila* may be disgusting, putrid, but announces itself as such; there is no disparity between inside and outside. The bad smell is a warning, an advertisement of its internal nature. By contrast, the *talmid hakham* without *da'at* seems to be other than he is – he claims, or his appearance does at least, that he is something else. He is the kind of person about whom Shakespeare's Thersites will say, 'most putrefied core' – righteous appearing, corrupt within. But he may give the credulous the wrong impression; there may be even those who will emulate his performative religiosity, thinking a screwdriver-wielding guy in a suit is *talmid hakham*, a wise Jew.

The Torah reveals itself or, through our engagements in this world, we reveal Torah in its many aspects, as we heed the call of the moment. Had the overzealous father bothered to look at the face of the 'birthday boy' – as his screw-driver was poised over that icing-crafted caboose on the cake – he might have paused. Had he emulated Moses, and been attentive to the demands of the moment, things might have turned out differently, with other kosher birthday cakes in the future, other children ready to take their portions.

7 Identity is out!

In a little over twenty-four hours I was told several times: 'No more identity!' First, I received a review of a book I coedited on the eighteenth-century British proto-feminist, Mary Astell. The reviewer in the *English Historical Review* laments that my coeditor and I treated Astell as – get ready for this – a woman. Go figure. But to our reviewer, Astell is just a *writer*, and to call her a woman writer is to make invidious distinctions showing a failure to move into a 'post-modern framework for discussing gender.' For postmodernists, apparently, androgyny is in, gender out.

Not only comments about gender identity, but Jewish identity also raised objections, in this case, even more strenuous. Referring to Woody Allen's Jewish *neshama* on my blog was construed as exclusive and maybe even racist. Not believing in a DNA test for the *neshama*, I never do argue for a genetic Jewish soul, but for a *neshama* sustained through Torah, tradition, and history. Yet, to some of my readers, I had made 'invidious distinctions' – that phrase again – between Jews and non-Jews.

Finally, the email from a friend about an academic project with what I thought an apt title: 'From Athens to Jerusalem.' He warned me, 'If you don't want to look like an Orthodox Jewish apologist, you better avoid the distinction between Athens and Jerusalem, and certainly that between Truth and *Emet*.' The Apostle Paul's notion that 'Jew is Greek and Greek is Jew' has become very popular in academic circles. 'You cannot and should not' – he now inveighed – 'talk about Jewish identity; you will be accused of being parochial, unenlightened, and narrow-minded.' He was accusing me of as much without even mentioning 'invidious distinctions.' All this is what the former *Commentary* editor Norman Podhoretz refers to as the 'scandal of Jewish particularity,' once a scandal arising from the outside world *about* Jews, now internalized *among* Jews themselves as an embarrassment.

Another friend confided quietly to me when I induced him to talk about his Jewish affiliation: 'I am nothing,' confessing an acute version of the embarrassment of the particular. He was embarrassed by *any* possibility of identity. Perhaps it is a cultural ailment of the postmodern age; in any event, it is one which Jews and Israelis in particular suffer from most. Arthur Neslen's *Occupied Minds*, advertising itself as a 'journey through the Israeli psyche,' provides its own fantasy of contemporary Jewish identity, or *non*-identity, living out the anxiety of particularity. Neslen, who provides insights into 'the Israeli Jewish mentality,' writes that he had wanted to conclude his book with an interview with 'some stoned Israeli on a beach in India' who 'had lost any connection with Jewish identity.' But he ends instead with a picture of Israeli stoners 'playing on the beaches of Ras a-Satan in Sinai' with fellow 'artists' from Cairo and Lebanon, gathered to 'drop their used skins and learn from each other.'

Of course, sometimes those skins, the external markers of identity are used as pretexts for malice – sexism, racism, all forms of prejudice. But the instinct to abandon identity – 'I am nothing' – almost certainly has its parallel dangers, like those detailed in Nathan Sharansky's against-the-grain *Defending Identity* where denial of identity is linked not with postmodern freedom, but Soviet-style fascism. Identity may be, as Sharansky writes, necessary for modern democracy. But more than that, without the starting-point of the self, and the external markings that sometimes really correlate to our inner worlds, all of the open minded encounters with difference may come to nothing.

In Genesis, God forms man 'from the dust of the earth.' Rashi provides seemingly incompatible explanations of the verse: that God gathered the dust from 'the four corners of the earth,' and that 'God took the dust from the altar of earth,' the sanctuary at the center of Jewish worship. But Rabbi Joseph Soloveitchik understands the variant explanations as testimony to the dual conception of man. Created from the dust of the 'four corners of the earth,' man is 'a cosmic being,' not a 'stranger to any part of the universe.' As citizen not only of the world, but of the universe, he breaks out of constraints, prejudices and parochialisms. This man, like Neslen's postmodern heroes, 'loves the cosmos'; 'he wants to be everywhere.'

But there is another aspect to man: the dust from which he was created has a source in the earthen altar at the center of the world, Jerusalem. He is the man of particularity, 'a rooted being,' not 'cosmopolitan, but provincial.' Rooted to his soil, as well as his service, this part of the human personality is reluctant to give up his inheritance. For Rabbi Soloveitchik, the two apparently conflicting types complement one another, parts of the hybrid self created in Eden: the man who wants to travel, but also the man who knows the value of his home. To recognize man's origin in the altar of the earth exclusively shows single-mindedness; while only acknowledging human origins – and destiny – in the four corners of the earth is equally impoverished. As Rosalind, in Shakespeare's *As You Like It,* remarks to the cynical and jaded traveler Jacques: 'A traveler! By my faith, you have great reason to be sad. I fear you have sold your own lands to see other men's; then to have seen much and to have nothing is to have rich eyes and poor hands.'

When we sell our own lands and our inheritance for the thrill of change and for a curiosity about the cosmos at the cost of forgetting home, we risk losing ourselves in an ocean of undifferentiated experience. This, Rabbi Soloveitchik writes, is how Cain lived, a 'restless vagabond' cursed to wander from one end of the earth to the other. Knowledge of the cosmos intensifies and deepens our experience of home, to be sure. But with home forgotten, the cosmos becomes a desert. And we do not even realize it. So we end up, with the sometimes fashionable embrace of nonidentity, having seen much, but left sad, desolate, and empty-handed, like Neslen's postmodern heroes stoned on the beach, wasted in the Sinai, tending towards oblivion.

8 Isaac's bad rap

During a six-month stint in Los Angeles – I was on sabbatical at UCLA – there was a Saturday morning *bar mitzva* in the local synagogue. Before the 'hot *Kiddush*' – *cholent*, kugel, and herring, more than I would ever eat for lunch at home – the rabbi spoke. First words on the weekly Torah reading, then about the family – I was already shifting in my seat – and finally the inevitable praise for the *bar mitzva* boy. 'David is a special boy,' the rabbi began – 'Uh-oh,' I thought, 'this does not sound promising' – because 'he is a good listener, and able to take advice.' *Nebekh*, pathetic: is that really the best the rabbi could come up with? True, it is a Jewish school, so the boy is not going to be captain of the lacrosse team or head of the student council, but a good listener? Able to take advice?

But then I thought of Maimonides' description of the patriarchs, Abraham, Isaac, and Jacob, and how, in that account, Isaac gets only the briefest mention. In the telling, like in the Genesis story upon which Maimonides relies, Abraham takes center stage: the forefather's youth in his hometown, *Ur Kasdim*; his rebellion against the idolatrous culture of his family; the trials he suffered; and the journey to the Land of Canaan, which becomes his inheritance, the Land of Israel. Maimonides writes that in the course of Abraham's travels, he attends to the questions of skeptics and doubters, and gathers 'first cities and then kingdoms,' teaching the principle of 'the One Everlasting God' – monotheism, remember, is an innovation, not a given. Maimonides devotes 266 words to Abraham's story, but just eight words to Abraham's son Isaac. He then devotes almost a hundred words to the life of Jacob. True, Maimonides is known for brevity – but for Isaac, just eight words? Is he also just overlooked, the middle and ignored patriarch?

'And Isaac sat.' Even Maimonides' few words about Isaac stress his passivity. Isaac, Maimonides continues, 'taught, and was careful' – the word '*m'hazir*' also means 'was cautious or circumspect' – and then, and this is the extent of it, Isaac instructs his son Jacob to pass on the tradition that began with Isaac's father, Abraham. For Maimonides, Isaac is who he is not for what he does, but by his presumed inactivity, for what he does not do. Abraham, for Maimonides, as in Genesis, is overflowing with *hesed*: he is the man of 'excess,' writing books, traveling, and teaching. But Isaac does not write books; he does not even leave the Land of Canaan. Abraham turns outward; Isaac is passive and inward. Isaac is the chosen son, the first in the tradition that begins with his father. But within that tradition he seems the passive middle-man between the two active patriarchs, not a man who goes out into the world, but the one who withholds himself.

When T.S. Eliot chooses the model for the 'classic,' it is not the Greek poet Homer – the first and original classic, and the seemingly obvious choice – but Homer's Roman follower Virgil. Does Eliot really prefer Virgil's Latin imitation to the Greek original? Maybe – but it is not Eliot's poetic preferences, but rather his idea of classicism that counts. For Eliot, a classic is not the work that begins a literary tradition, but the one that allows for the tradition's continuity. Homer is the beginning; but Virgil brings the Homeric inheritance into his contemporary Rome, as well as the European future. True, Virgil's story borrows much – almost everything it sometimes seems – from Homer. But, for Eliot, keeping the past alive to be passed on to future generations is what makes a classic, an activity that falls to the later poet, Virgil not Homer. The 'most individual parts' of a poet's work, writes Eliot elsewhere, 'may be those in which the dead poets, his ancestors, assert their immortality most vigorously.' A poet is at his most original when most traditional – counterintuitive to be sure – when the past speaks through him.

Abraham is also a beginning. But his *hesed*, the excess of giving, does not make for tradition. Isaac represents the limitation, the restraint or withholding that makes tradition possible. So, in Genesis, Abraham's servants dig wells, which are later filled by the Philistines. Isaac may not be an originator, but by going back to the past and the wellsprings of Abraham, he preserves the tradition of his father, as he re-digs the wells giving them the name that his father gave them.

In this relationship, Abraham needs Isaac as much as the latter needs his father; there can be no tradition of Abraham without the more conservative and disciplined efforts of the son. This discipline means, in Eliot's terms, nurturing a 'historical sense' – of going back to the past not just to blindly follow it, but to find new resources for the creative self. For Eliot, 'tradition' and the 'individual talent' are not opposites, they come together. In the Jewish tradition, the excess and restraint of the two first patriarchs allows for the Torah of Israel, realized fully in the third, the House of Jacob, the people of Israel. Jacob brings together the excess of creativity and the restraint that allows such creativity to have a future, for tradition.

The tension born out of the relationship between Abraham and Isaac comes to life in the second-century sage Rabbi Eliezer ben Hycarnus. A field hand on his father's estate until the age of twenty-eight, Eliezer never studied Torah. His father found him crying in the fields: 'If plowing on the hard ground is too difficult, then maybe you would prefer to plow on softer ground?' 'No,' cried Eliezer, 'I want to learn Torah.' Unsympathetic, his father answers, 'Marry and raise children of your own; you can take them to the House of Study. But in the meantime, get back to work.'

Instead Eliezer goes to Jerusalem to the academy of Rabbi Yohanan ben Zakkai. During the years of his study, he sits quietly. Years pass: the day arrives when Eliezer's father, weary of his son's indulgence, travels to Jerusalem to disinherit him. Upon his arrival, he finds all the sages gathered; Rabbi Yohanan places him at the head table, and asks his student, so long silent, to say words of Torah. But Eliezer is reluctant: 'I am like a cistern from which you cannot draw more water than has been put into it.' So, he continues, 'I cannot say more than I have received from you, my teacher.' I have nothing to say which you have not taught me.

But Rabbi Yohanan responds: 'You are not a cistern, but a spring: and as a spring produces more than flows into it, so your Torah will exceed that which you have received from Sinai.' 'Open,' commands Rabbi Yohanan, 'and expound for us.' 'I cannot open.' Rabbi Eliezer replies.

'Perhaps you are embarrassed in my presence,' answers Rabbi Yohanan, as he moves to stand behind his student. Eliezer accedes, uttering words of Torah that had never before been heard or even imagined. As Eliezer expounds, his face glows like that of Moses upon his descent from Mount Sinai. And so Rabbi Eliezer, the one who receives and listens, and personifies the passivity of Isaac – the vessel that does not lose a drop – becomes like the greatest of prophets, Moses. Though Rabbi Eliezer is insistently modest, he himself becomes a great original, a *m'haddeish*, an innovator. Rabbi Yohanan understands his student's modesty so he stands behind him. But it is because the teacher is behind the student, and not just literally, that the latter is able to be an original. Rabbi Eliezer becomes what the poet John Donne calls a 'potent receiver,' both passive and active at once. Even what looks like passivity, just receiving, is part of the creative act.

Part of the independence of creativity is the desire to receive, to be a cistern like Rabbi Eliezer, to acknowledge not knowing, and to nurture both the passivity and discipline that are part of creativity. 'Open up your mouth wide, and I will fill it,' God says to King David. In the translation of the nineteenth-century rabbi, Samson Raphael Hirsch, God says, 'Open up *your desire*.' Opening to the past is an act of disciplined attention, but also reveals a desire to be part of it. Eliezer's tears of desire – 'I want to learn Torah' – turn into the words of Torah that flow from him, transforming him from a cistern into a spring. So Isaac returns and attends to the wells of his father and opens them so that future wells of Torah may flow. In the next verse in Genesis, the servants of Isaac dig new wells, and find *mayim hayyim*, living waters. The receptivity of desire, of wanting to connect with the past, as the *bar mitzva* boy who is merely good at taking advice, is also part of the creative act, letting the 'living waters' of the past nourish present and future.

9 Cheeseburger

I am tempted by the smell of cheeseburgers.

There, I said it.

I also sometimes pine after the taste of a spicy pork sandwich that I ate at a café on the Greek island of Samos, before I started to keep kosher, in the summer of 1988.

Say something like this at a *Shabbos* afternoon meal, and witness the metamorphoses of otherwise self-possessed seminary girls, like Odysseus's men on Circe's island, transformed by facial contortions, gaggling noises, and squealing sounds of disgust: '*Ichh*!'

Rabbi Elezar ben Azariah asks, 'From where is it known that a person should not say "I am repulsed by pulled-pork-barbeque sandwiches," or "I do not want to wear that Armani woolen suit with a linen lining," but rather a person should say, "I really want these things, but what can I do, my Father in Heaven decrees that I must not?"' He answers with a verse in Leviticus: 'And I will separate you from the nations of the world to be Mine.' For Rabbi Elazar, God does not separate the people of Israel from the nations through mystical decree or genetic fiat, but the Torah provides instructions to the Jewish people for how to separate and distinguish themselves. As Rashi explains Rabbi Elezar: 'You, the people of Israel – *through adhering to the Torah* – will separate yourselves for My Glory.' Your actions, not your being or essence, make you separate and holy.

The command to Israel to separate itself from the nations of the world comes at the end of the weekly portion *Kedoshim* which, Rashi explains, was taught to all of the people of Israel – men, women, and children – because on its principles the rest of the Torah depends. In a weekly portion that begins by exacting 'you shall be holy' – understood as distancing oneself from illicit relationships – Rabbi Elezar insists that when it comes to observing God's heavenly decrees, or 'ordinances,' He wants the people of Israel to be honest about their desires. These ordinances have no rational bases; they are observed because they are the decrees of the King.

'Do not walk in the ordinances of the nations of the world,' God commands, 'but rather you shall keep *My* ordinances.' My ordinances, and not theirs: the nations also have *hukkim*, rendered in the Aramaic translation of Onkelos as conventions or social norms. Not just the people of Israel abide by the strict decrees that *hukkim* represent. All cultures – from Athens in the ancient world to my hometown in Long Island – abide by social forms, not necessarily rational, accepted without question and from which one does not readily or happily divert. In the time of the sages, for example, it was participating in the culture of 'stadiums' and 'theaters' (sound familiar?) that was *de rigeur*. *Hukkim* are what every one does, because, you do not have to ask, that is just what *you do*. They are literally *engraved* on the heart, accepted and unquestioned social conventions. Of course, in every nation, there are also things you just *do not* do. The people of Israel have their *hukkim* as well, not subject to rational explanation, but, in this case, they are decrees of the divine. To separate from the nations means, in the first instance, avoiding their practices and conventions, but also abiding by *hukkim* in a way that is distinctive. If I simply strive to get in line with accepted norms of social behavior – blurting out, like the seminary-girls at the table, 'OMG, I hate pork!' – I turn God's will into etiquette advice, or use the Torah to justify my already determined preferences. But God is not Emily Post.

The service enjoined by the Torah is different. So Rabbi Elazar stresses that God's act of separation – 'I have separated you from among the nations' – requires a parallel act of separation by the Jewish people: the people of Israel 'must separate themselves from transgression.' Rabbi Elazar says that the Torah requires honesty about desire, and the acknowledgment that in the absence of *hukkim*, we would most certainly do otherwise. The Torah shows the people of Israel crying at the 'doors of their tents' – because, according to the sages, they had just heard the divine decree prohibiting certain sexual relations. The Torah is not embarrassed to show what the people of Israel really want.

Not only do unrecognized desires lead to split-personalities and pathology, but only acknowledging desire makes the act of separation significant. We are not scandalized by our desires, treating them like pictures in an old photograph album to be hidden away from the children; but we make them part of our service. To say that my desires are already in line with the will of God may appear righteous. But ask Rabbi Elazar: that is a performative religiosity, not what God wants. To the contrary, refraining from *paella* and the latest Italian fashions and claiming it is natural is a way of following the nations, not performing an act which shows service to God. Through acknowledging desires and refraining in any event, one distances from transgression, enacting separateness.

But if we claim to find things repulsive which are really desirable to us, then we are – because of overzealousness – becoming more like the nations, and less like the chosen servants of God. God wants our separateness, but to fulfill the command, 'You shall be holy,' to be truly separate, we do not enact a robotic observance, but acknowledge our humanity even as we perform God's will.

10 Writing an inspirational story

I recently connected with an old friend; we had been in high school together, though not in the same class. Justin recognized my name: 'I knew a Billy Kolbrener when I was in high school.' That is how I was known back then, but when we met, he could not link my name to my face. Over *café hafukh* at David's Citadel in Jerusalem, we discovered similar paths taken. Though many of our fellow classmates in high school maintained strong Jewish identities, only Justin and I, with a few others, overcame the suburban aversion to observance – avoiding the term orthodoxy – to discover what Justin described as the 'treasures' of Judaism. He was not talking about the tunnel tour near the Western Wall or the laser show on the Old City's Walls.

In our conversation, Justin confided that he had an interest in inspirational stories of people who had overcome challenges as they maintained and strengthened their faith. In Jerusalem, there is no shortages of such stories; I hear them all the time. The previous day, a friend recounted a *hesped* from a funeral service he had attended. Sparse in recounting of the facts of a life: from a birth in Austro-Hungary, to a loss of parents in Auschwitz, to the beginnings of a life in France, to an eventual re-settlement in the United States and then Israel. This was the story of a woman's life, or what seemed to be different lives, interspersed with the challenges and tragedies that someone from my comfortable background can hardly imagine.

My thoughts turned also to the pair of men who sit in front of me in synagogue – 'regulars,' always precisely on time; 'early is also not on time,' one of them often chides. More than sixty years ago, they had been among the children of the *Kindertransport*, German Jewish children who were sent away from their homes by parents who had intimations of what was to come. 'Imagine a mother,' my older friend related, 'sending an eight-year-old on a train, knowing she would never see him again.' He was envisioning, in a different time and different continent, the trauma that he had experienced himself, but displacing the emotion onto a mother he barely knew. Brought on one of the special trains from Germany which carried children during the period that began shortly after *Kristellnacht* and ended with the *Blitzkrieg*, they were 'relocated' with British families, many of them not Jewish. The two bonded as young refugees in England as the war spread and the fate of their parents was sealed. At war's end, they were separated – one remained in England, the other went to the United States – until they were reunited in a small synagogue in Jerusalem, my neighborhood *shul*. In my neighborhood alone, there are hundreds of such stories, of resilience in the face of adversity, the kind that Justin wanted to read.

Stories as these do not fail to make an impression, but I was struck, by the end of our meeting by another story – Justin's. By any measure, Justin was successful, having risen to the top of his profession, with access to all of the accoutrements of luxury, wealth, and privilege which his position afforded. For Justin, to the mixed admiration and disapproval of friends and relatives, had made his own sacrifices, given up many of the benefits and entitlements, moving with his family to a community with a synagogue, placing his children in Jewish day school, and committing himself to a life of service to God and others. In Jerusalem, he was visiting schools, orphanages, and hospitals, dispensing checks, while many of his colleagues may have been vacationing at Club Med.

The Baal Shem Tov teaches that the approximately six hundred thousand letters in the Torah correspond to the six hundred thousand who gathered on the foot of Mount Sinai at the time of the giving of the Torah. To the hasidic master, every Jew has his or her corresponding letter in the Torah. The task of a lifetime – the psyche is connected to the Torah that nurtures it – is the discovery of that letter. No letter is the same. Though some contemporary purveyors of inspirational stories seem to claim otherwise, there is no 'objective' template for Torah observance. King David's counselor, Ahitophel, the sages say, wore all of the outward trappings of a devout Jew, but God rejected his service, because the service was not his own. God wants the whole person – that is, he wants subjectivity to express itself *in* and *through* service. Ahitophel did not search for and write his own letter, but imitated the service of others. 'Give us our portion in your Torah,' we beseech God, a portion which is not merely waiting for us, but which we have to make. So God wants our letter, not that which belongs to someone else. We may gain strength and inspiration from the letters of others, but we should also own up to both the challenges and pleasures of writing ourselves.

God forms the world, the kabbalists write, through three things: '*sefer,*' '*sefer,*' and '*sippur*' – two books and a story. The first two are the books of the world through which God reveals himself, the book of the natural world, and the book of the Torah. The third is the means of self-revelation, the story that each person writes for himself. God's overarching story is tied up with the stories – the letters – we make for ourselves. But these letters cannot be found ready-made, our stories cannot be written by others. True, making too much of ourselves leads to egotistic self-satisfaction and stagnation; but making too much out of the stories of others may come from a performative and forced humility leading to resignation and the inability to find and write our letters.

In Jewish practice, the absence of a single letter from a Torah renders it invalid: for the Torah to show itself fully in this world, each Jew needs to find his or her own letter. Once found, we spend a lifetime crafting that letter, writing our letters for all to see. Sometimes, it is true, it takes someone else to see the beauty of the letters we have already begun to craft, to feel the inspiration of the stories we have started to write.

On our way out of the hotel, as Justin and I walked through the revolving doors of David's Citadel, he turned to me with a sudden recognition and said, 'You are the Billy Kolbrener I once knew; when you smiled, I recognized you; it is you!' People like Justin and I find inspiration in the stories of great and righteous people, maybe even the biographies found in religious book stores. Though sometimes we may also find evidence of letters in unanticipated places, and in recognizing them, discover how those letters are shaping us and others in ways we had not expected.

11 *Eros* and translation

On the Sabbath of the Passover holiday, I borrowed a friend's English translation of the Song of Songs. Some read the Song of Songs every Friday evening; in my synagogue, and many others, we read the Song written by King Solomon the Sabbath morning after the Passover *seder*. God redeems the people of Israel on Passover; we celebrate the intimacy of that relationship through reading the Song of Songs.

All of the songs of the Hebrew Bible, says Rabbi Akiva, are 'holy,' but the Song of Songs 'is the holy of holies.' The Song records the passion of two lovers – which the sages understand as the relationship not between flesh and blood lovers, but between God and His people Israel. The 'holy of holies' is the innermost sanctum of the Temple; God's love for His chosen nation is the secret that lies behind the poetry of the Song.

My Hebrew is far from perfect, but before too long, I realized that what I was hearing in synagogue bore little resemblance to the English version I had in front of me. The Artscroll Song of Songs, my borrowed translation, gives the 'allegorical translation' rather than a literal rendering of Solomon's words. Other editions of the Song put the interpretation of the sages in the notes. Artscroll, however, puts the 'literal meaning' in the notes, with the allegorical reading imported – not an easy feat for the most able of translators – into the translation itself. Artscroll has been providing English translations of traditional Jewish works since 1977; and they have been praised for capturing the '*zeitgeist.*' But does the 'spirit of the times' of Artscroll's translation reflect the sensibility of the work they translate into 'allegory'?

The second verse of the first chapter of the Song begs a comparison. King James offers: 'Let him kiss me with the kisses of his mouth: for thy love is better than wine,' rendered by Artscroll as 'Communicate your innermost wisdom to me again in loving closeness.' Not only clunky and abstract, Artscroll also erases the passionate physicality, the *eros*, from the work. The King James translators – here, the

Cambridge Company of translators led by Francis Dillingham – show why the 1611 translation of the Bible is the most Hebraic of works in the most Hebraic of periods of English Literature. They do not shy away from presenting the physical, even the fleshly meaning of the original Hebrew, for they *also* understood that the tangible world serves to express the divine. Adam Nicolson, in a book on the King James Bible, writes that the superficial and surface style of the American World Bible recalls the atmosphere of a '1930's bathing party.' Artscroll evinces not a bathing party, but a philosophy seminar where mention of the body might seem uncouth, vulgar.

Poetry does matter; King Solomon, after all, as well as rest of the prophets, often writes in the language of the poetry. So claiming the poetry of the Song 'has no independent validity,' and pushing it, with the plain meaning, to the bottom of the page obscures the 'deeper meaning' Artscroll means to convey. King Solomon might have chosen any metaphor to show Israel's longing for the divine, but he represents Israel's exile, and her desire for a return to the God through the estranged lover yearning for a former intimacy. Recollections of the closeness of revelation, of God speaking to Israel on Mount Sinai, are, says Rashi, the longed-for passionate kisses. And to Rashi – whose interpretation Artscroll follows – the 'kisses' are not just rituals of politeness, a peck on the cheek or a ceremonious kiss on the back of the hand, but kisses on the mouth. Even as Rashi gives his allegorical interpretation of Israel's longing for the 'face to face' encounter with God of former times, he stays close to King Solomon words. Without the concrete images of Solomon's poetry, the allegory is made abstract – 'thought,' as T.S. Eliot writes disparagingly of certain trends in English poetry, 'without feeling.'

The longing for the intimacy of the divine is not strictly intellectual, but sensuous as well. With its allegorical translation, however, Artscroll separates thought from feeling, rendering, for example, the verse King James gives as, 'Thy two breasts are like young roes that are twins,' as 'Moses and Aaron, your twin sustainers, are like two fawns.' Solomon likens the desire for closeness with the divine through the longing for a nursing mother's breasts, only then compared to a connectedness with God's most faithful servants and teachers, Moses and Aaron. Artscroll, however, makes the image literal – Moses and Aaron as 'sustainers' – an image verging on the absurd, and preempting the process of reading by passing over the poetry to provide only the 'deeper meaning.'

For Rabbi Akiva, the Song of Songs is the 'holy of holies.' But in order to arrive at the holy of holies in the physical architecture of the Temple, one has to pass through the courtyard designated as 'holy.' To get to the holy of holies – the reciprocal love between God and Israel – one has to first pass through the 'holy,' the *eros* of Solomon's song. But Rabbi Akiva does caution, 'Who ever sings the Song of Songs in banqueting houses and turns Solomon's Song into a "*zemer*" or drinking song loses his portion in the world to come.' Only reading the song in the right place, in the right frame of mind allows the passing from the 'holy' to the 'holy of holies.' Read the poetry of the Song in synagogue or in the House of Study, but do not turn the Song into a pop song – a '*zemer*' – and in the process, diminish it. Do not listen to it on an iPod, but listen to it as a 'song,' and proceed from the 'holy' to the 'holy of holies.'

Maimonides, the so-called 'rationalist,' in his work devoted to repentance, describes love of God as 'love sickness,' the love of a man for a woman, the source for which is the love described by King Solomon in the allegory of the Song of Songs. Acknowledging *eros* and passion may be not be sufficiently 'religious' for some in the current cultural climate, but Maimonides understands that the 'deeper meaning' of Solomon's words are only fully understood or *felt* through experiencing the poetry of the Song.

'Torah,' Rabbi Joseph Soloveitchik writes, 'does not address itself to the theoretical man, or the intellectual,' but rather 'to the person who is relating to and sharing in something.' 'Taste and see that the Lord is good,' writes the Psalmist. Worship is not merely cognitive but physical (the Artscroll translation – no surprise here – goes not with 'taste,' but the more abstract 'contemplate'). Relate and share, partake, not with just with the mind, but the senses as well. The poetry of what Rashi describes as 'the passionate dialogue between lovers' leads to 'the story of the evolving relationship between God and Israel.' But the latter story, without the yearning of the former, presents a disembodied religion of passionless ideas, turning reading the Song of Songs into a cognitive exercise. Our relationship to God, however, is not merely intellectual. God wants not only our minds, but our desires as well.

And He wants us to remember that Song of Songs is a love story.

12 'Swaying towards perfection': Torah, worldliness, and perversion

Perversion, Adam Phillips writes, involves 'an anxious narrowing of the mind when it comes to pleasure.' What defines sexual perversion for Phillips is the 'determined sense of knowing' what one wants. 'The person in a perverse state of mind,' Philips writes, 'has no conscious doubt what will excite and satisfy him.' Knowing what one wants, and fixating on the fulfillment of a specified set of expectations – this is the sensibility of the perverse mind.

Even generous readers may be wondering what Phillips' notion of perversion might have to do with Torah – no matter how open-minded. What could be wrong with the certainty of knowing what one wants?

Rabban Gamliel, the son of Rebbe Judah the Prince, says, 'The learning of Torah is pleasing when accompanied by *derekh eretz* or worldliness – for toiling in both of them causes sin to be forgotten. The study of Torah which is unaccompanied by labor will come to nothing and lead to sin.'

Engaging with the physical world – 'worldliness' and earning a livelihood – leads, the Maharal writes, to the perfection of the body; studying Torah leads to the perfection of the soul. For the temptations of the body for licentiousness and the temptations of the mind for idolatry, work and Torah provide the respective antidotes. But the former takes precedence. Not only, or even necessarily, working a nine-to-five job, but engaging with the world is the necessary pre-requisite for Torah. The character traits essential to *derekh eretz*, or worldly engagement – a considered and considerate way of being in the world – are not mentioned in the Torah, writes the Vilna Gaon, because they are assumed: without them, Torah is impossible.

Both kinds of engagement, the Maharal emphasizes, require what Rabban Gamliel calls 'toil' or exertion. Such toil holds out promise; its opposite brings about stagnation. Everywhere the Torah mentions 'settling,' the sages write, there is eventual failure and disappointment. When the people of Israel '*settled* in Shitim,' they soon gave themselves to licentiousness – 'and the people began to commit whoredom with the daughters of Moab.' After Jacob '*settled* in the Land of Canaan,' the patriarch's favored son Joseph is sold into slavery. The people of Israel *settle* in Egypt, and soon after, Jacob, here called Israel, 'approaches the end of his days.' For the sages, settling breeds stagnation, selling off of the future, and eventually death.

Pursuing the perfection of body and soul through worldly engage-ment *and* Torah study protects the self from, in the Maharal's terminology, the forces of 'privation and lack.' The paradox is that rest, entertaining a perfection already achieved, opens one up to negation and loss. When one is 'moving towards,' or more literally in the Maharal's phrasing, 'swaying towards perfection,' then one is immune to the sin that attends the belief that one has already arrived. Swaying toward a perfection never to be achieved in this world protects one from transgression. 'He who thinks we are to pitch our tent here,' Milton writes in *Areopagitica*, 'that man shows himself to be very far short of the truth.' He who claims to have reached truth, by that very assertion shows his distance from it. So for the sages, the premature proclamation of having arrived at truth is a form of stagnation or death.

Clinical perversion is the expectation of the fulfillment of vulgar expectations, of pitching my tent and hoping to never leave, knowing what I want – and planning that my future will be just like my past. The perverse act, as Phillips writes, is one in which 'nothing must be discovered.' Perversion is not just an attitude toward the fulfillment of physical desire, but a stance taken toward the world in which I already know what I want. Not only individuals, but communities, even a gen-eration, can suffer from such perversion. So, while we think to know the direction in which we are headed, when we claim to have arrived, or to already be 'in the know,' we are already lost in the perversion that foreshortens life. The acknowledgment of lack, however, another paradox present in both Milton and the Maharal, shows perfection. The frantic certainty, by contrast, of a perspective achieved is a mark of failure, the cover story for self-doubts about facing the demands of discovery.

The Torah provides a set of instructions for such discovery, an impetus and framework for striving, the means by which immersing ourselves in the past we live in the present to create a new future. The *hiddush* – the innovative interpretation in the House of Study – is an ideal not only in the learning of Torah, but in one's way of life, in worldliness, as well. To Rabban Gamliel, one needs to toil – to be fully engaged – in both. Foreclosing discovery with expectations that the future be merely a copy of the past – through insisting that stereotypes are models and clichés ideals – leads to settling and stagnation, the perverse selling-off of the future. Swaying toward perfection, and acknowledging a goal *never* to be attained promises, by contrast, an undiscovered future of engagement, and with it, the possibility for change.

13 Jacob's scar: Wounding and identity

The most famous scar in Western Literature belongs to Odysseus. Disguised as a beggar, he returns from the Trojan War to Ithaka. To prove his identity to his few still faithful servants – he has been away for twenty years – he shows his wound. Not his driver's license, or his college ID, but the scar on his thigh. Odysseus's wound and identity are linked.

'What's in a name?' Shakespeare's Juliet asks Romeo: 'Would a rose by any other name smell as sweet?' For Homer, as for Shakespeare, the answer is no. Odysseus's name, linked to his wound, is central to his identity. His grandfather, Autolycos, in the Homeric version of the *brit mila*, names him: 'Just as I have come from afar, creating pain for many . . . so let his name be Odysseus, the son of Pain.' Autolycos gives a name meaning literally both to suffer and to cause suffering, and as happens so often in the Greek world, Odysseus lives out the fate of his name, suffering, causing suffering, and winning glory. As a young man, he hunts a wild boar that gouges 'a deep strip of flesh' over his knee. The young Odysseus finally triumphs over the beast; and when he returns to his parents, he 'tells his tale with style' of how he got his wound, bringing glory to himself. Years later, returning home disguised as a beggar, his old nurse, Eurycleia, washes him. Only after she runs her hands over the groove of the wound does she cry out, 'Yes, yes, you are Odysseus!' For Homer's hero, the wound and identity are one.

But there are other famous wounds, other famous scars.

Fearing the vengeful wrath of Esau after having taken the birthright of their father Isaac, Jacob sends emissaries to his brother with gifts; takes special precautions for his family; and finds himself alone on the banks of the Yabok river in the middle of the night:

And Jacob was left alone; and a man wrestled with him until the break of the day. When the man saw that he did not prevail against Jacob, he touched the hollow of his thigh; and Jacob's thigh was put out of joint as he wrestled with him.

The sages say that the 'dust' which whirled up from these two wrestlers 'rose up to the Throne of God.' Not an ordinary wrestling match, Jacob strove, the sages say, with the 'ministering angel' of Esau. The battle, as Rabbi Samson Raphael Hirsch explains, provides the prototype of a struggle that continues through history, marking the beginnings of the 'world-historical struggle' between Jacob and Esau, Israel and the culture of the West.

In this struggle, Jacob also suffers a wound; his thigh was 'put out of joint,' *dislocated*. But the story continues: 'The sun rose upon him as he passed Penu'el, limping because of his thigh.' So Jacob limps through history. In the end, the sun does shine '*upon him*,' and the healing light promises an end to painful trauma, the experience of dislocation – suffering and exile. Jacob's wound, like that of Odysseus, is important to his identity: it is the wound that marks his exile, but it is also tied to a change in name.

Esau's ministering angel grants Jacob a new name: 'Your name shall no longer be Jacob, but Israel.' No longer Jacob – the one, as the sages say, 'who comes from behind' – but Israel, who even Esau acknowledges as the rightful inheritor of the blessing of Abraham and Isaac. Esau had wanted to destroy Jacob, and declare supremacy for all time, but Esau 'could not prevail against him.' Jacob may limp through history under the shadow of the powers of Esau, but even Esau acknowledges that the end of history promises a dawn in which the sons of Jacob, that is Israel, will be blessed: 'And he blessed him there.' But that blessing does not come to pass at once. After their meeting, Esau travels directly to Mount Seir, the seat of his inheritance. Jacob, by contrast, builds a *sukka*, a temporary structure, anticipating the path of the people of Israel, a path of wandering, first in the desert, and then through history.

Odysseus uses his wound to win glory and a name, as he does again with the one-eyed giant, the Cyclops. Again following the fate of his name, Odysseus first suffers at the hands of the Cyclops. But then

Odysseus inflicts pain, driving a burning spike into the crater of the eye of the giant, and owning up to his name, brings glory to himself: 'I am Odysseus.'

Jacob's wound is different. Following Jacob's triumph over Esau's 'guardian angel,' God commands him to abstain from eating the '*gid ha-nashe*' – the sciatic nerve of the cow. '*Nashe,*' Hirsch writes, means weakness or vulnerability. Odysseus suffers and brings himself glory through retelling his exploits and naming himself; Jacob is commanded to embrace the law of the 'sinew of weakness,' foregoing the physical strength of this world.

Esau, like Odysseus, is 'a cunning hunter, a man of the field.' The sages call him 'snake thigh,' for in the place Jacob suffered his wound, Esau bears a different mark, an image of the snake. Esau bears the imprint of the primal snake that deceived Eve with the promise of divinity – 'You shall be as God.' Whereas Jacob's wound is a reminder of creaturely imperfection, Esau is adorned with the image of the serpent, the sign of the false promise of worldly perfection. Esau, in his physical prowess – the sages tell us that he was born with hair, fully-formed – does not recognize the infirmities of others. The law of the sinew, bringing glory to God in its observance, reminds Jacob to embrace his vulnerability, not forego it. But embracing the law of the 'sinew of weakness' is not only a way to refuse the powers of Esau and the desire for immediate glory and power. Jacob's wound is also a way of showing that the strength of Israel comes from elsewhere, not from the physical powers and glories of this world, but from the observance of the divine command that bears him through history and exile.

When Esau invites Jacob to 'come with me,' Jacob refuses. Instead, he 'leads on softly,' accommodating the pace and needs of his cattle and 'tender' children. Jacob will one day fulfill the fate of his name, Israel, when the dawn breaks, at the end of history. But, for the meantime, he is Jacob, the one who comes from behind, who is incomplete, and who lacks. So Jacob leads on softly.

The wounds of both Jacob and Odysseus show that loss and suffering are tied to human identity. Not as René Descartes would have it, 'I think therefore I am,' but 'I have lost and suffered, therefore I am.'

In response to that suffering, Odysseus pursues his own glory. Jacob pursues the glory of Heaven, all the time recognizing his own vulnerability, which allows him to acknowledge the tenderness of others and repair an imperfect world.

14 Torah and the pleasure principle

A kosher atomic roll in Manhattan in the eighties? *Fuggetaboutit!*

These days, Jews looking for a community will as likely judge a potential new home for its kosher sushi as for its synagogues and ritual baths. It was different when I was in graduate school: 'You mean you are not only giving up Friday nights at the West End Bar, but sushi as well, and the breakfast special at the Mill Café, that also?' The list went on. All of the restrictions, the dos and don'ts, endless considerations of what the poet George Herbert calls 'what is fit and not' are of *your* making. If you want to make yourself crazy, 'fine,' my friend said; he might have quoted the poet: 'He that forbears/ To suit and serve his need,/ Deserves his load.' 'If you want to make yourself miserable, I'm not going to bother,' he said with a shrug: 'it's your life.'

He was not just referring to the pleasures of dark beer and raw fish. To him, I was taking on religious restraints, and avoiding the more urgent demands of the creative self. He might have quoted Freud's *Future of an Illusion*. 'Religion,' Freud writes, 'is the obsessional neurosis of humanity.' And the Jews, for Freud, who in this regard were worst of all, act out their own dramas of neurosis through ever more 'strict observance,' falling prey, as Robert S. Paul writes, 'to a collective obsessional neurosis, namely, Judaism itself.' For Freud, obsessive observance and the avoidance of pleasure are symptoms of the super-ego gone crazy, the Jewish way to punish the self, and in the process avoid its deepest needs.

Following Freud, the anthropologist Joseph Campbell cataloged the mythologies and rituals of world cultures, celebrating the ones he most admired, like the Hindu Upinshads. In the process, Campbell made famous the phrase, 'follow your bliss.' In Campbell's cultures of preference, in which the Jews are notably *not* included, following your bliss is not a call to pursue shallow physical pleasures, but to pursue the demands of what the psychoanalyst D.W. Winnicott calls the 'True Self' – the authentic self, creative and individual. Knowing all this, I realized that behind the offer – 'Coming out for sushi tonight?' – was the question made possible by Freud and Campbell, 'Can you be Jewish, and follow your bliss?'

A day for the denial of the needs of the self – a midwinter fast on the tenth day of the Hebrew month of *Tevet* – gives an unexpected opening to understanding Jewish pleasures. Most fast days commemorate events that led up to the destruction of the Temple in the Jerusalem; the tenth of *Tevet*, no exception, marks the beginning of the siege of Jerusalem by the Persian King Nebuchadnezzar in 586 BCE. But the date also marks an event for which Jews once fasted not one day but three, the translation into Greek of the Five Books of Moses. At the command of King Ptolemy, the seventy members of the Jewish Sanhedrin were compelled to translate the Torah, producing the 'translation of the seventy,' the Greek Septuagint.

From Walter Benjamin to Bill Murray, we know that things get lost in translation, but it still may be hard to understand the sages' aversion to the Torah in Greek. After all, God commands Moses in Deuteronomy to translate the Torah into seventy languages so that generations in exile, not knowing Hebrew, will be able to return to their inheritance. But fasting in January, after *Hanuka*, is not a fast over a Greek Torah scroll, rather what Ptolemy did with the translation, taking the Torah out of the House of Study, and putting it in the *gymnasia,* his version of the university library. Ptolemy gave the Torah the Hellenist version of a Library of Congress call number, and in so doing gave it the same status as other books in the Greek library. 'Study the Bible in the university library,' Ptolemy says, 'but do not learn Torah in the House of Study.' In the library, the Torah could be 'gazed at by all' – not only Greeks, but Jews as well. Ptolemy began the process of turning the Jews into the 'People of the Book' – not a native Jewish concept – making the Torah external to them. The fast after *Hanuka* marks the time when Jews became enlightened outsiders to their tradition, unemotional 'objective' observers, distant and disengaged.

I am no stranger to either the library or the House of Study. In the library – at least when things go well – I have mastery over my research. Writing my dissertation on John Milton in Burgess Carpenter Library at Columbia, I arranged and rearranged stacks of index cards – a long time ago – into just the right order. But the study of Torah, or rather 'learning Torah' involves not mastery, but a readiness to be addressed, to enter into a relationship. Learning with a *chavruta*, a study-partner, attentive to him as well as the Torah, entails a willingness to give up mastery, and place oneself at risk. 'You talking to me?' Robert DeNiro's anxious question in Scorcese's *Taxi Driver* stands as a response of someone in a relationship who knows he is being addressed, and, even more threatening, perhaps being asked to change. Torah asserts relationship; Ptolemy undid that relationship, seeking to turn Torah into something neutral and abstract.

When the Greeks contemplate – and, in some sense in the West we are, as the Maharal writes, all Greeks – they do so in visual terms. Greek theory, or '*theoria*,' translates into Latin as *speculatio*, or speculation, understood in the Renaissance as 'a sight' or 'a beholding.' Greek wisdom comes from the perspective of gazing and standing outside, in which sight takes priority. In giving a Jewish hierarchy of the senses, the thirteenth-century sage, Rabbenu Yonah of Gerondi, turning to Proverbs, finds not seeing, but hearing to be the most important of the senses. 'The light of the eyes makes the heart rejoice,' writes King Solomon, 'but a good report fattens the bone.' Hearing, Rabbenu Yonah writes, is of greater importance than seeing because it makes the heart – beating, alive – rejoice. Hearing gets to the core of a person, even the bones. Sight may quicken the already-beating heart, but hearing penetrates and enlivens the bones.

For the sages, the priority of hearing, as Rabbenu Yonah shows, has an unexpected source, the laws of damages. If Reuben causes Simon to lose his limb, an arm let's say, the former must pay the 'market' value of the arm. Causing loss of sight obligates payment for the value of the eyes, while damage to hearing, resulting in deafness, requires the value of the whole person. To be sure, the sages understand that life and limb cannot be quantified in any ultimate sense, but these rulings serve the purpose of compensation. In the Talmud's sometimes intricate discussion of injury, the Maharal finds a question similar to one that both Aristotle and Shakespeare's Hamlet ask: 'What is man?'

For the sages, however, man is not a political animal, or a rational animal, but man is a man by virtue of his being able to speak and *hear*. In the Aramaic translation, Onkelos renders the word for hearing as *kabbala*, meaning receiving or internalizing. So the centrality of hearing in Jewish prayers, '*Shema Yisrael*': 'Hear O Israel' focuses on a message not just cognitively understood, but internalized. For knowledge in Torah is not based upon objective distance and neutrality, but rather upon a connectedness, not only achieved by the mind, but heart and bones as well.

When the sages of the Talmud argue, their positions are attributed with the phrase '*a-liba de*' – meaning 'according to.' Literally '*a-liba de*' means 'according to the heart,' a prepositional phrase showing the distance between Jewish and Greek tradition. For, as early as in Plato's *Republic* centuries before Ptolemy, heart and mind are already sundered, with the Socratic distinction between 'rational principles' and 'pleasure.' But the sages of the Talmud think, as it were, with their hearts. So a sage is a *haver*, not only literally a friend, but one who joins and who is *m'habber* the people of Israel to Torah, to each other, to God. From this perspective, the sages' counsel – *aseh lekha rav* – 'make for yourself a teacher,' is not just practical advice to find someone to answer questions about how to make your oven kosher or to observe the Sabbath, but an injunction to cultivate a relationship. The sages do not say *find* a teacher – look up someone in the phone book – but the more active '*make* for yourself,' make the effort to connect to a tradition that began on Mount Sinai. Solicit relationship, not independence and neutrality.

That entering such relationships entails even the greatest risk – to identity – is illustrated in the sages' account of the giving of the Torah on Mount Sinai. With every one of the divine utterances that began the relationship on Sinai, 'the souls of the people of Israel left them, only to be revived, each time, by an angel.' With each divine utterance, their souls left them and their identities were transformed. Neuroscientists have shown that from one instant to another, the brain not only changes, but is entirely nonidentical to its former state. Mount Sinai was a scene not of what neuroscientists today call 'neuro-plasticity,' but rather *neshama*-plasticity, showing the capacity of the *neshama*, or soul, to change, to suffer a metaphorical death – their souls escaped them – *and* become anew through the imperative of connection and relationship. What from one perspective may look like constraint or restriction, from another is engaged connectedness, with all the risks and opportunities it affords.

Years after I declined an invitation for sushi on the Upper West Side, my brother called me in Jerusalem from Boulder. He was about to take his two boys to the NBA All-Star game in Denver. Not only had I deprived myself in the past, I thought, as I hung up the phone, but now I am depriving my son of similar pleasures, the 'Shaq Attack!' But the game passed, and on the following *Shabbos*, Moshie, then about twelve, vanished toward the later part of the afternoon. When he returned after sunset, I asked, '*nu*, where were you?' – my annoyance at his lateness held back at the sight of his smile. 'I was at *Sha'arie Tzedek*,' the hospital about a twenty-minute walk from our house. 'In the hospital?' I asked. 'I was visiting Shlomie; don't you know he had his appendix removed?' I was relieved. 'And you were. . . .' Moshie stopped me mid-sentence: 'I was doing *bikkur holim*,' performing the *mitzva* of visiting the sick. So that was the smile: this was the pleasure of connectedness, not only with his friend, and with God – the root of the word *mitzva* is connection – but with me as well, in the evident pleasures he had in telling his father of a good deed done. I will not deny the pleasures of the Shaq Attack – nowadays I might suggest we Tivo the game – but Moshie's smile was a sign not just of constraints, but of connectedness, and a different kind of pleasure.

Part II Dispute and community

15 Oedipus in a *Kippa*

At the beginning of Sophocles' tragedy *Oedipus Rex*, a chorus of elder priests surrounds the shrine of Apollo. Fallen, broken men, they mourn the plagues that have befallen their city Thebes, lamenting that the gods have abandoned them. Oedipus, who had already saved the city once, evidences sympathy for his people: 'I would be blind to misery not to pity my people kneeling at my feet.' Lauded by the elders as a 'chief of men,' he commands the devout priests: 'Don't pray to the gods; pray to me. I will grant your prayers!' Jocasta, his wife – and as we know too well, his mother – is distraught, skeptical, mocking the oracles of the gods and their supposed involvement in human affairs: Come off it, Oedipus, she scoffs, 'Chance rules our lives,' she tells him, advising him to forget the gods and their oracles and to 'live as if there is no tomorrow. Seize the day.' Oedipus, by contrast, shows himself certain in his knowledge of the gods, as well as the ability to enact that knowledge: 'I am Apollo's champion!' I know what the gods want; and I will be the one to perform their will.

But in Sophocles' terrifying vision, you cannot know – even when the gods seem to be talking to you, revealing their will. This is what the psychoanalyst, Jonathan Lear, calls 'the other Oedipus complex': the belief in the certainty of knowledge, that you always already know, not only the present, but the future as well. The chorus is the exception in Sophocles' play: trusting Oedipus's power, they proclaim their lack of knowledge and powerlessness, part of the traditional culture the enlightened Oedipus wants to leave behind. In the end, the worldview of the chorus is vindicated: the gods are all-powerful in ways that are incomprehensible. Apollo prevails but not in a way anyone had imagined, least of all Oedipus. Oedipus is a victim of his certainty – perhaps this is what Aristotle means when he writes of Oedipus's tragic flaw of hubris or arrogance – his confidence in his knowledge of the gods, and that he is the one to bring about their will.

Imagine an Israeli production of *Oedipus Rex*, with the chorus as ultraorthodox in their long black *bekishes* and flowing *pey'ot*, the skeptical and secular Jocasta in a pants suit, and Oedipus wearing a knit *kippa*. The modern public sphere in Israel has its versions of the knowing Oedipus: the ultraorthodox, national religious, and even secular, all proclaiming programs for redemption, as they scramble to define the public sphere, and bring the Jewish people to what Kent in *King Lear* calls the 'promised end.' Even with the shock of the Lebanon War and the disengagement from Gaza, the national religious version of Oedipus still claims to know the divine will and to be able to enact it, proclaiming their own version of 'we are God's champions.' The spectacle of the Israeli army removing settlers from their homes may have undone some of the mythology of 'Greater Israel,' but the inheritance of the Six-Day War, when Israel really seemed an extension of the divine hand, remains resilient. The natural religious, however, are not the only ones with a messianic agenda. The secular have an ideal of the public sphere, which is, if no longer the Zionist state, then at least a state informed by the progressive and liberating forces of enlightenment. And the ultraorthodox – whose skepticism should make them demur from these grandiose visions of this-worldly redemption – betray their principles by mixing politics and religion with attempts to fashion the public sphere in their own image. All of these are maximalist, strong, and exclusionary visions, revealing another Oedipal fantasy: 'I must rule!'

Perhaps it is time to forgo this other Oedipus complex, and to strive for a public culture in Israel stripped of the competing extremist dreams. In this proposal, everyone loses something, but it may be one, in the end, where everyone wins. Ultraorthodox skepticism about the state means acknowledging Israel as a modern nation state in which one has obligations as well as rights. The national religious give up on their vision of the immediate realization of the divine promise of redemption in history. The secular forgo their sometimes exclusionary and intolerant vision of progressive enlightenment. What survives is a conception of Israel as a modern Jewish nation state offering not redemption, but providing protections and rights, a Jewish multiculturalism.

By comparison to the dreams of redemption, the benefits are admittedly limited. The national religious gain a more inclusive sense of community – of secular and even ultraorthodox – who see themselves as fulfilling a more modest version of the zionist dream (note small case z), a zionism without pretensions. The secular gain a public sphere based on principles of genuine inclusion – they can be more faithful to the liberalism they advocate – and a universalism generally open to difference. The ultraorthodox gain membership in a State, divested of its messianic aspirations, as well as the possibility for economic mobility which that membership entails.

What everyone gains is a noncoercive public space for self-reflection and a conversation that in the process may lead to the realization: we have more in common then we had thought. The elders in Sophocles' play are devoted citizens of Thebes; Jocasta – the seeming skeptic – sneaks away to pray to the gods. So we might discover that the ultraorthodox – think of the *nakhal haredi*, the ultraorthodox unit of the Israel Defense Forces – value the State and citizenship; and as a recent poll shows, those Israelis who consider themselves to be 'secular' feel the 'deep pull' of God's promise to Abraham. All of us, like Jocasta, have secrets hidden away in our closets. When not pursuing the strident and exclusionary visions, we may find ourselves open to those aspirations which we have secretly harbored, making it easier to identify with those we thought to have despised. True, newspaper editors in Tel Aviv and billboard makers in ultraorthodox neighborhoods make it more difficult to break out of the dance of codependency and hatred. But there is a growing sense that the sociological categories and languages of enmity that sustain fanatics of every color have run their course, that there is a need for new ways of talking, thinking, and acting, reflecting the diversity of life and culture beyond the headlines in *Haaretz* and the billboards in *Me'ah She'arim*.

The immature dreams – fantasies perhaps – are discarded, but an admittedly more minimalist and inclusive set of possibilities emerges.

Here is a place to invoke the philosopher Hilary Putnam: 'Enough isn't everything, but enough is enough.' Maybe it is time that Israelis from across the spectrum all begin to settle for enough.

16 Open minded Torah I: Judaism and fundamentalism

Someone called me an 'ultraorthodox fundamentalist' today. To make it even worse, he said I am 'biased out of my brains' – and this is not the first time. When I was a graduate student in the English Department at Columbia, after not showing up one Friday at the West End Bar, and soon after seen in the corridors of Philosophy Hall with a *kippa*, I heard whispers, and even, the 'f-' word. Not '*frum*' – what they might call me now, if they were generous, and knew Yiddish – but fundamentalist or fanatic. Had I embraced any of a number of perspectives – postmodernist, Marxist, feminist, or psychoanalytic, or as Shakespeare's Polonius might have put it, postmodernist-feminist-psychoanalytic-deconstructionist – I would have been embraced without reservation, but the skull-cap in the seminar room did not play well.

Friends expressed both disbelief and disdain – 'So you've taken up the crutch of religion'? They wondered about what they thought must be my abandonment of pluralism, difference, and complexity – a sure sign, for Mark Edmundson, a biographer of Freud, of the religious fundamentalist. Was my desire to connect to that image – my great-grandfather Velvel glancing up from under his hat – religiosity veiling obsession, or just a nostalgia verging on fanaticism? Is there a place between fundamentalist adherence to religious authority and the 'skepticism of everything' that goes under the name of postmodernism?

The Talmud recounts a dispute between Rabbi Eliezer and the sages. In the course of an argument about the ritual purity of an oven, Rabbi Eliezer calls out to the Heavens: 'If the law is as I say, let this carob-tree prove it!' On cue, the carob-tree is ripped from the earth. The sages are not impressed: 'You can't bring any proof from a carob-tree.' Rabbi Eliezer persists, showing a full range of special effects at his disposal: a stream of water leaves its course; the walls of the House of Study in which they stand begin to topple. Throughout, the sages remain unmoved. Finally, the lone sage calls out: 'If the law is as I say, let it be proven from Above!' A Heavenly Voice calls out: 'Why do you argue with Rabbi Eliezer since in all matters the law goes according to his interpretation?' On the book jacket of Rabbi Eliezer's *Shulhan Arukh*, his code of Jewish Law, is a blurb from God: 'He's right!' Notwithstanding the divine plug, the sages are unconvinced.

When Zeus, in Virgil's *Aeneid*, sends Mercury down to Aeneas who is loafing in Carthage with his lover Dido rather than building Rome, the epic hero does not say, 'Sorry Zeus, I'm busy adorning the buildings of Libya.' Aeneas heeds the Olympian voice, and gets up and goes to found Rome. But in the Talmud's story, even though Rabbi Eliezer has God's backing, the other sages counter: 'The Torah is not in Heaven!' 'The Torah has already been given on Mount Sinai,' they explain: 'We no longer listen to a Heavenly Voice.' Rabbi Eliezer has the best claim to the Truth, but the sages are unconvinced, making Judaism a strange fundamentalism, if one at all. Not only does truth, after the giving of the Torah, 'sprout from the earth,' as the midrash affirms, but truth is also plural, a result of interpretation and disagreement.

The Talmud records another dispute, between the Houses of Hillel and Shammai: 'For three years, they debated each other; the former said that the law is in accordance with their view, the latter that the law is in accordance with theirs.' Finally, a Heavenly Voice calls out, 'these and these are the words of the Living God.' The Houses of Hillel and Shammai are not, however, arguing about aesthetics – to which we could add the modern qualification, 'beauty is in the eye of the beholder.' One says the equivalent of 'the hamburger is kosher' while the other says, 'it's *treif*, not kosher.' It is about this kind of dispute, not disputes about taste or preference that the Maharal writes, God proclaims, 'these and these are the words of the living God.'

Medieval interpreters of the Talmud may have been reading Aristotle and his 'law of contradiction': 'x is true' and 'not x is true,' writes Aristotle, are incompatible statements. So Ritva of fourteenth-century Seville wonders about the dispute between the Houses of Hillel and Shammai: how can the same thing be at once permitted and forbidden? How does God say of opposing, indeed contradictory, perspectives, 'these and these are the living God'? To answer, he cites the French sages of the previous century: 'When Moses went up to Mount Sinai to receive the Torah – he was there for forty days and nights – God revealed to him forty-nine ways to forbid, and forty nine ways to permit on every question.' That is, Moses received a Torah already including the opposing perspectives that would be available to later generations.

In the sixteenth century, Maharshal, Rabbi Solomon Luria, gives a different solution to the problem of the Heavenly Voice. God says 'these and these' because each of the sages perceives the world in 'accord with his own capacities,' and 'the unique character of his soul.' Ritva stresses the complexity of the revelation on Mount Sinai; Maharshal, the perception of those who received it. From a contemporary perspective, with fundamentalism and postmodern relativism the only options, Ritva becomes the advocate of the objective truth of fundamentalist orthodoxy, with Maharshal becoming a hero for a postmodernism celebrating the individual. In the all-or-nothing scenario, there is either the whole – absolute – truth or no truth at all, relativism. It all already happened at Sinai, or, alternatively, everything is up to individual interpretation, and 'anything goes.' In graduate school, one classed oneself either with the professors who believed in truth, authority and tradition, or those defending individual interpretation, difference, and pluralism. To one, the others are the barbarians at the gates; while to the latter, the others are fascist, fanatical authoritarians. But, before the traumas that have fostered a Jewish world of polarized extremes, the dispute between the Ritva and Maharshal comes as itself one of those disputes about which is said 'these and these are the words of the living God.' The alternative approaches are placeholders for an emphasis, *not* a position. The Torah was given by God on Mount Sinai, so Ritva stresses; but it was also, in Maharshal's emphasis, given to the people of Israel. Torah comes into being in the world only by means of this relationship.

To compare great things to small, look at the figure you may have already seen in a perceptual psychology class, or a philosophy seminar on Wittgenstein, or on a menu at a fast-food restaurant.

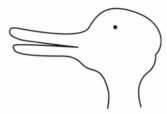

The brave guinea pig in the lecture hall will volunteer, when asked to describe the image – 'It's a duck.' But flipping it ninety-degrees, to the anticipatory giggles of the rest of those present, reveals a new perspective: 'Oh, it's a . . . rabbit!' This is the shock of the unexpected, seeing something new.

But what is this picture *really*? Calling it a 'duck/rabbit picture' is one option, but, as psychologists have shown, it is only seen at any one time *either* as a rabbit *or* a duck. Describing his experience, the common sense philosopher Ludwig Wittgenstein writes, 'Now I'm seeing it as a duck,' and after, 'Now I'm seeing it as a rabbit.' He doesn't say, 'it *is* a duck'; for it is only a duck when he sees it as such. Everything depends on perception.

But, 'these and these' is not just an inclusive principle, allowing for pluralism – and making the sages, in, as in the claim of a Reform rabbi, postmodernist liberals before their time – but also an exclusive principle. So the inference: 'these and these,' but *not* those. The drawing sustains interpretations of 'duck' and 'rabbit,' but to someone calling out from the back of the hall, 'it's an elephant,' we will say, with sensitivity but firmness, 'Sorry, but you are wrong.'

'There are seventy faces to the Torah' – another principle of the sages that is both inclusive and exclusive. Seventy may be many, but it is not an infinite number. In the process of learning Torah, there are the equivalents of ducks and rabbits, but also elephants. Like the duck/ rabbit picture, the Torah – though allowing for different perspectives – also places limits upon what it is possible to say. The Torah yields different faces, depending, as Maharshal writes, upon the capacity of the one who sees, but the Torah does not sustain *any* interpretation. As Ritva stresses, something happened on Mount Sinai that constrains future possibilities for interpretation. There are those who claim to reveal faces of Torah – ducks and rabbits – when all they show are the elephants of their own imagination.

Emet, the Hebrew word for truth spelled with the letters *aleph, mem,* and *taf* – the first, middle, and last letters of the Hebrew alphabet – is an inclusive truth of different perspectives, distant from what we often think of as *the* Truth. 'These and these' is not reducible to categories of subjectivity or objectivity – the generally fruitless way people in the West often argue about truth. Rather learning Torah is an engaged attentiveness to the revelation from Sinai, governed by the 'laws of perspective,' nurtured through a sensitivity to complexity and difference – no fundamentalism there – in the framework of commitment and belief.

17 Irony *Über Alles*: An episcopal passover

In a blog entry posted in the *New York Times*, 'This I Believe,' Judith Warner reflects on an unconventional religious upbringing. Though she identifies herself as Jewish, for nine years – from age five – she attended an Episcopal school. She would never call herself a Christian, but 'her heart,' she admits, 'sings to the organ chords of the Doxology.' Citing Darwin's *Descent of Man* to explain her 'not altogether reasonable' religious proclivities, she explains that those like her, embracing 'a post-modern form of faith' are 'defined by little bits and pieces of experience and belief that together form a mosaic that for us, at least, is coherent and whole.' Finding coherence in disparate parts of experience against the resistance of skeptical critics – this I found compelling, as well as the belief in a hybrid self, accommodating the demands of different voices within.

There are a lot of people, Warner confides, who view her faith – as well as that of a 'striking number' of her friends – as 'confused.' 'Some of us just can't find a home for ourselves in the categories of identity that make sense for other people.' I could relate, especially in a Jewish world where categorical mania – 'What color is his *kippa*?' 'What length is her skirt?' – is pervasive. But what starts in a confessional mode, a call for tolerance for idiosyncratic choices, turns, by the end, into a preachy rant against those who do not embrace her idea of what it means to be religious. The implicit message of 'This I Believe' is that if you don't thrill to the prospect of a Jewish-Catholic-Episcopalian *seder*, or to a long weekend of combined Passover-Easter activities; or to children who are so hip that to their mother's invitation to a religious service – this time Unitarian – they respond, citing the conquest of the Incas, 'I don't want to be part of it,' then there really must be something wrong with *you*.

For Warner, ironic distance reigns in her version of the hybrid self, a personality allowing for anything *except* commitment. Warner remembers the Passover *seders* of her parents and grandparents, skipped pages and the 'prayers' (though the *hagada* is a story, not a prayer) 'read *ironically*.' There should always be a place for irony, but for her and the friends for whom she writes, irony is the only place, the only available point of view. There are other versions of irony, providing perspective within a framework of commitment. But for Warner and her 'motley crew' commemorating events that 'they don't believe in' – who would want to do that anyway? – there is only the fashionable version of irony, excusing a disengagement that masquerades as sophistication.

I do not begrudge Warner her experience – the hymns, and stained glass windows, and polished silver. But please do not speak for postmodern faith or as an authority for the rest of us. There are those of us who may also consider ourselves postmodern, but aspire to a form of faith and religious service – where is service in Warner's theology? – that transcends an eclectic feel-good aestheticism. Without the inner springs and deep emotions which Warner rightly celebrates, there may not be much to religion and faith. But there may be more as well than just the personal 'mosaic' – like possibilities for community, connection, and meaning born out of a sense of duty.

Writing with the confidence of a faith she imagines would be approved by Darwin, Warner affirms that the world of her parents and grandparents is 'dead' while claiming indifference to her children's refusal to join her in religious observance – 'I don't care what they say.' Notwithstanding what she claims, however, I also have a striking number of friends for whom their religious tradition is still living. For them, and me, *mesora*, tradition, literally 'passing on,' is central to an experience which is not abstract and solitary, but lived and shared. This vision involves both parents and children, past and future, coming together, as well as the aspiration, to paraphrase Freud quoting Goethe, of taking the inheritance of ancestors and making it one's own.

Included in these friends are those, also trying to make sense of the bits and pieces – the hybrid voices – of their postmodern experience. They may prefer the almost majestic look, utterly *without* irony, of a great uncle, with *matza* on his shoulder at the beginning of the *seder*, circling the table, exclaiming, 'With haste we left from Egypt.' Or the concentration, also without a trace of irony, of the youngest child, as she clears her throat, *hagada* in hand, readying to ask 'the Four Questions.' Or the earnest voices of the remaining children, after having found the *afikoman*, the last pieces of *matza* at the end of the *seder*, who can be heard singing '*Had Gadya*,' late into the Jerusalem night.

18 Of false kabbalists and conjurers: Parenting and idolatry

My daughter missed her bus this morning. I suspected as much. When I looked up from my oatmeal, I noticed uncharacteristic bickering with her sisters, and characteristic dawdling. With a cup of orange juice in her hand, and the promise to drink it on the way to the bus, she rushed out of the house.

A few minutes later she was back, the cup of juice in hand, half-full now – I wondered if she had drunk it or if it had spilled as she ran to the bus: 'I missed my bus.' Surprise. A long pause, and then: 'Mommy, will you drive me?'

My wife had an exercise class, and after that a *shi'ur*, a lecture she had helped organize at a friend's house. 'I'm sorry, not this morning. You'll have to get to school on your own.'

My daughter sank into the couch; she pouted. I went to my office to gather my things.

When I came back – my wife had now prepared juice for me as well – our daughter even deeper in the recesses of the couch: 'I am not going to school!' A good opening, and then: 'There's a test tomorrow, and today is the only day to study.' Another dramatic pause: 'I am going to fail, and I don't care!'

'Is this grapefruit juice or pomelino juice?' I asked my wife: 'It tastes unusually sweet and delicious.'

Now, from the couch, the tears: 'I am going to fail my test,' and, the stakes raised, 'I am never going to school again!' I felt for her; seeing the tears stream down her face, I was tempted to drive her myself.

In the earliest months of life, Winnicott writes, an infant relates to the world as just a part of him, not something separate. The infant has no real conception of self, or of others' selves, not even his mother. Mother and infant are 'merged,' Winnicott writes; when the child is hungry, the mother fulfills his needs. This early scene of omnipotence – with the infant 'conjuring' the presence of the mother and her appearing as if by 'magic' – serves, Winnicott writes, an important part of development. Through fulfilling his desire, the mother allows the infant to both have an experience of himself, and encourages his creative engagement with the world. Through 'being seen' by his mother, and having his needs recognized, the infant begins to have an identity.

But the illusion of omnipotence gives way – or at least it should – to acknowledging a world beyond the infant's control, starting with a mother who, over the course of time, becomes more than just a part of the infant's fantasy conjured at will, but a separate person. The child learns that the world is not just an extension of his desires; and he starts to recognize signals that come from without. This signaling, Winnicott writes, anticipates – is the beginning of – what becomes in the adult world, communication. Winnicott's 'good-enough parenting' takes the infant from his fantasy of control over a reality with which he feels united to the possibility of relationship. True, identity always bears the traces of early childhood. But adulthood does not mean communion, but contact with a world acknowledged to be distinct and separate.

'I am sorry you missed your bus, and I don't want you to fail your test, but you are going to have to find a way of saving your day by yourself. Do you need money for the bus?'

My daughter had tried to conjure my wife and me. The tears and cries and threats were attempts to elicit a primal connection, though we did not give in. The night before I reminded her, she had been in my place, trying to persuade her younger brother Pinhas to eat the peppers from his salad so that he could have the Ben and Jerry's Chocolate Fudge Brownie in the freezer. '"If you don't eat your peppers, no ice cream"' – 'that is what you told Pinhas.' Pinhas did his own conjuring act, not with tears and protests, but cajoling smiles and kisses. 'Kisses and ice cream later,' she had said: 'First your peppers.'

'There shall not be magicians among you' – so says God in Deuteronomy to the people of Israel. The prohibition of magic is severe, writes Maimonides, because of its kinship with idolatry, for those who 'conjure' aspire to harness forces in the world independent of God. Today there is a whole culture of false kabbalists and conjurers, claiming to elicit connection through magic – investing things with spiritual powers, like the red string bracelets which Madonna wears, or 'kabbalistic jewelry.' Of the latter, there is even a 'soul collection' that boasts of accessing 'creative forces' in the universe, promising easy communion with the divine. Some 'religious' people will insist that *segulot* – special 'lucky' practices, charms, or incantations – create a connection to God. But these inclinations only reveal a desire to return to what Freud calls the 'blurring of boundaries' of infancy, that original primal unity between mother and child.

Judaism wants a different form of connection, not through communion, or even mystical union, but relationship. The God of Judaism, the French philosopher, Alain Finkelkraut writes, enjoins the breaking of idols and the 'disenchanting of the universe.' There are no spiritual shortcuts for connecting with the divine. 'Clear out the idols,' God says. He does not inhabit the world, nor are there magical forces which allow for such communion: that is the sensibility of idolatry to which magic is akin. Only when the world is emptied of idols – atheism may be closer to Judaism than idolatry – does the possibility of a different kind of connectedness come into being.

Abandoning the idolatrous practices of magical conjuring is the precondition for the relationship made possible through the revelation on Mount Sinai. Revelation allows for a holiness that does not inhere in people, places, or things, not activated through special charms or practices, but one that comes through a relationship established through speech. A space cleared, without idolatry and magic, allows for responsibility and choice. *Mitzvot* – which means both the commandments that God gives and the actions which the people of Israel perform – has, we remember, the word *tzevet* at its root, to join. Through *mitzvot*, there is the joining with God, not by communing with Him, but coming close to Him, through heeding his words. Infancy is the idolatry of the illusion of magical omnipotence; adulthood the renunciation of idols and magic and opening the space that allows for communication.

Encouraging children in their attempts at magical conjuring, the acts to elicit intimacy, denies the more refined closeness that comes through distance and speech. The 'good-enough mother' accedes to the early fantasies of omnipotence of her child, but only as part of the process of developing a self capable of relating to a world outside. 'Two distincts, division none.' Real closeness, as in Shakespeare's poem, depends upon a similarity based upon difference. I need to have a sense of self and the other – and the space between us – to experience a more refined union. Communion creates an illusion of closeness that in reality is only the continuation of the narcissism of infancy. This may be the fate of the child without 'good-enough parents,' arrested development and the nourishing of illusions of magical omnipotence, not the cultivating of a sense of self and others based upon connectedness.

I might have been conjured by my daughter. But I reminded her instead, as she secured her backpack walking out the door to catch the bus, that there are better ways to connect. 'Pinhas really did enjoy his ice cream in the end, didn't he?' With that, I gave her a kiss, and she went off to school.

19 From Sinai to the Uzi: New and old Zionisms

There is something about the Arrivals Hall at Ben Gurion Airport outside of Tel Aviv that gets to me – maybe I compare it with the dreary arrivals building at JFK, another gateway for immigrants. Getting to the airport early allows more time for watching the distinctive Ben Gurion spectacle, where airport guards seem less interested in security than overseeing family reunions. For me, it means greater leisure to embellish the stories of the arriving passengers: the high school girl back from her first trip abroad, her fifteen gathered friends with a giant welcome sign; the high-tech executive returning from Silicon Valley to his wife and balloon-bearing twin daughters; the squat Bukharin women walking tentatively as their Israeli flag-waving family, sighting them, let out peals of joy. The financial pages of the newspapers express a common fantasy: if only all of the Jewish CEOs and Hollywood entertainment moguls would make *aliya*, then the Israel economy would really prosper. But I do not fantasize about George Soros and Stephen Spielberg in Israel; I would rather welcome friends and relatives. 'The Torah has seventy faces,' say the sages: so, I often think, does the Land of Israel. So when a friend showed up at the Arrivals Hall at Ben Gurion, I looked forward to his new face on Israel, and a visit together the following afternoon to the Israel Holocaust History Museum, Yad Vashem.

In any museum it is difficult for me to concentrate long on the exhibits. I morph into the impatient adolescent version of myself. But in Yad Vashem, even for people like me with low museum-tolerance, there is more going on. Like the exhibit of a pre-war Viennese living room – with dining room table and embroidered wall-hangings – abandoned in the late thirties, but now filled, in awkward triumph, by *kippa*-wearing soldiers in their green khakis, looking as if they stumbled into the wrong movie. And in the Auschwitz galleries, an American in a Boston Red Sox hat volunteered to no one in particular: 'If any one has any questions, my father can answer,' pointing to the man beside him, 'He was there.' And the girl in the Def Leppard T-shirt – an unlikely figure for mourning – with one of her iPod earplugs dangling, crying in the Hall of Names.

If that was not enough to keep us busy, there was also, like many great contemporary museums, the architecture of the place, and, in the case of the building opened in 2005, the contrast with its predecessor. You can still see the old museum from the sixties, the two-panel sculptural frieze adorning the blockish building's outer walls. On the right is the image of a procession of Jews, weak, shrouded, and downcast, the Jews of exile and the ghetto, at the center, a Moses-like figure, bearing a Torah scroll. His hands may be raised, but the Torah seems heavy in his arms, the upward gesture not making him, or those with him, look any less dejected.

The frieze on the left – the Hebrew-reading mind moves from right to left – gives a different vision, of a Jew no longer downtrodden, but standing upright, noble and triumphant. The cylindrical centerpiece of the previous tableau, the Torah scroll, is replaced by the barrel of a machine gun: the modern Israeli bearing the weapon, bare-chested, hopeful, and strong. Although the second sculpture was commissioned to commemorate the fighters of the Warsaw Rebellion, the frieze became part of a 'before and after' story of the 'New Israel' told since the founding of the State. The 'before,' the old weak European Jew of the ghetto wed to the Torah and religious life; the 'after,' the new strong Israeli Jew, independent, defiant in his might and military strength.

In the new museum, not in a sculptural frieze, but in the architecture of the building, the before and after story is re-cast. Upon the triangular wall at the entrance that serves as one end of the long prism-like shape of the museum, scenes from the World That Was Lost, the Europe of before the war, are projected. In the grainy old images, a different, more complex story is told. There are still the pious Jews marshalling their horse-drawn carts down *shtetl* paths, but also Jewish trade unionist marching on expansive modern city avenues; in another image, there is an old synagogue, but also an adjacent library. Then there is the Hitchcock-like *Rear Window* sequence peering into windows of Jewish life: two women framed by a door sporting the latest Warsaw fashion; an older man seated at a piano practicing; a hasidic boy *fehered*, tested by his *rebbe*. Not the Jew of Europe portrayed in caricature, but rather a variety of Jews – like the community in the *Memorial Book* of Govorovo – a diversity absent from the image on the earlier museum frieze. What replaces the machine-gun bearing modern Jew of the second frieze, the 'after' part of the story is even more arresting. True, in the last exhibit hall, there are the children of Munkatch, bundled up in their winter coats outside of a school, singing what would become the Israeli National anthem '*Ha-Tivka*,' interspersed with the footage of Ben Gurion's 1948 declaration of the State.

But this more conventional Zionist ending to the story is off in one of the side galleries, subordinate to another one which becomes clearer when emerging from the dark low center of the museum into another brightening triangle, a set of windows, directly opposite the projected images at the museum entrance. Opening the glass doors set within – a burst of wind – to the expansive view of the Jerusalem Forest. 'Exhilarating,' my friend said.

One walks through the doors not to the polemical Zionist triumph of the old museum frieze – though there are those who continue to thrive on the tired antagonism represented there – but to the lowercase zionism of the horizon of possibilities. Turning away from the iconic story of Israeli military triumphalism, the victory of the present over the past, nationalism over peoplehood, the new Yad Vashem opens up a story for a zionism without idolatry, for a Torah which does not foster ideology but is the antidote. This is the zionism of the Land of Israel. Like the Torah revealed through its many faces: so with everyone who enters the Arrivals Hall at Ben Gurion, another face of Israel is revealed.

20 Modernity is hell: Korah and Hobbes

I sometimes wonder about historical figures to have at our *Shabbos* table; I think Thomas Hobbes, the seventeenth-century philosopher and author of *Leviathan*, would be a great candidate, though he would probably scare the children. He scares me! Hobbes, the first philosopher of modernity, saw, or better, he helped invent, a world of only bodies, just an interacting 'motion of limbs'. Though Hobbes devotes half of *Leviathan* to religion, he allows nothing beyond those limbs: just the physical world, nothing divine. Out of Hobbes's universe of physical bodies and their conflicting desires comes the need for the 'Leviathan' who through his 'rule by the sword' and brute power provides the only barrier to 'endless war', and the life of man described as 'solitary, poor, nasty, brutish and short'. Without God or shared beliefs in rationality, there are only competing desires and political interests: she may dress up her interests in one value system and set of beliefs and he in another, but everything always boils down to power, politics, and interest. The sensible person, or at least the one described by Hobbes, will say, 'with only warring passions and interests, best to give into the authoritative and authoritarian Leviathan, and let him keep the peace.' Without anything else binding people together, authority holds sway as Hobbes creates the modern commonwealth of power.

Enter Korah, the Leviathan of the desert. In the Book of Numbers, Korah questions the authority of Moses, the most humble of all men, God's true prophet. 'You are a politician,' he says to Moses, 'you have set up your brother Aaron in a cushy position as High Priest; your nephew as next in line; and you take the leadership position for yourself.' 'You are running,' he continues, 'a corrupt government based upon *protexia* [for non-Israelis, nepotism]; and you benefit most.' To win favor with the people, Korah transforms into the more egalitarian Spinoza and says, 'We are all holy, Moses; not just you; spread some of the power around.' Korah does not believe in 'Torah from Heaven' so he 'deconstructs' Moses: 'It's your doing Moses; your Torah keeps you

in control; your Torah reflects your preferences: you don't like cheeseburgers; you are of the levitical class and like the day of rest; that is
why you gave us this Torah of *yours*.' All Korah desires and wants is
power, so he sees nothing else, even in the selfless and humble Moses,
the servant of God.

The sages say that there are two kinds of dispute, one 'for the sake
of Heaven,' represented by the disputes of the Houses of Hillel and
Shammai, the other by Korah and his followers. The disputes of the
first type, the Maharal writes, are 'beloved by God' because both
parties are committed to Torah, not their own interests or ideologies.
The Houses of Hillel and Shammai learn Torah 'for its own sake,' not
Torah as a means to pursue separate and competing agendas. And
though they disagree – and sometimes say opposite things – they are
united through their love of Torah. That a voice from Heaven calls out
and proclaims: 'these and these are the words of the Living God' shows
that they are joined, their words affirmed, even in their disagreement.

The unity in disagreement that comes through learning Torah for its
own sake is made possible through what the Maharal describes as the
mystical power of the number 'three.' In three, two separate lines are
transformed into 'one' through a third line that joins them. Through
the Maharal's geometry, three is at the same time *less* and *greater* than
two. And Jewish algebra: three unites into the number numerically less
than two (that is, one); but the 'one' – really three – is superior to two
in representing unity.

Two becomes three becomes one. Korah however is forever stuck in
the realm of two in which, as the philosopher Alasdair MacIntyre
describes, there is only 'shrill' screaming, no meaningful disagreement.
To disagree, it turns out, is also an act of underrated difficulty. Korah
does not know how to disagree without hatred, and shows no interest
in a disagreement of common interest. The sages pair him not with
Moses, but with his fellow politicians and plotters, the company of two
hundred and fifty men, who follow Korah to their deaths. For Korah
does not pursue the unity which comes from a dispute for the sake of
Heaven, but a dispute for the sake of self-interest and division. The
medieval *Sefer Hasidim* says that 'when proven wrong in debates about

Torah, one should rejoice; but if you prove others wrong, do not rejoice.' The descendants of Hillel and Shammai rejoice in being proven wrong in a disagreement for the sake of Heaven. With the mystical number three, it is not the adversarial 'one against one' and the consequent hatred of enemies, but two united through the power of the third.

Korah's form of dispute was created on the second day of Creation, the day the waters above and below were separated (a cosmic division) – the only one of the six days of Creation which God does not call 'good.' It is also the day, the sages explain, when hell was created. Hell is division without the hope of coming together, of separation and absence, a vacuum filled only by the warring desires of men whose lives are 'nasty, brutish and short.' And so Korah projects a world based upon his selfish desires and political machinations. As Rashi says on the phrase 'Korah took' – Korah separated himself from the rest of the community in order to continue his dispute. But as Korah and his followers sink into the abyss of the fiery earth that swallows them, the rest of the people of Israel cry out, the sages say, 'Moses is True and his Torah is True.' The Torah of Moses makes possible a world where the division of two turns into the unity of three.

Hobbes describes a world many of us still inhabit, pervaded by power, politics and faction, self-interest, and endless division. This is a world of fragmentation, loneliness, and lack of connectedness. Korah's dispute provides a legacy for Hobbes which the latter has given to the modern world. In a word, Hell.

21 Lost and found

We lost our five-year-old son, Shmuel, who has Down syndrome. On a *Shabbos* afternoon, one of those days when the notion that *Shabbos* is 'a taste of the world to come' was in the air. We felt it in the street in front of our house, now without any traffic, a runway of families with sisters in matching dresses, yeshiva boys in their best fancy hats with their bags of sunflower seeds, and the flocks of chirping elementary school girls ('Oh, there's our Avital!'). Our little ones were out in front of the house experimenting with tricycles and scooters; my wife was chatting with some neighbors; I was on my way to synagogue for *mincha*, afternoon prayers. In our house, the cry 'Where's Shmuel?' is not uncommon, so when I heard my wife asking the girls first, and then the neighbors, I was not *that* alarmed. One gets attuned to such things: it is like knowing when the cry of a child after a fall means 'it's just another one of those falls,' or when it is a reason to raise the advisory level to 'code red.' But after the first set of search missions – in our apartment, on the steps in the building up to the roof (we once found him there), in the parking area on the ground floor – still nothing. No Shmuel.

We spread the web of our reconnaissance and enlisted more troops. Dusk was approaching, meaning both darkness and the return of traffic. So we spread out in all directions. My oldest son Moshie had come back from synagogue, bringing along some friends to help in the search. I had watched enough *24* episodes to know the importance of 'making a perimeter,' but I didn't know exactly where the perimeter should start – or is it end? How far can a five-year-old go in eight minutes? Pretty far, I thought to myself. Our neighborhood in Jerusalem is on the top of a hill so I ran to the bottom, wanting to make sure that Shmuel had not wandered somewhere he would not be recognized. As I hurried back up toward our house, still without Shmuel, I saw my wife walking toward me. I could tell – no longer the gait of panic – that he had turned up. 'So where was he?' Every parent asks a version of this

question; 'What did he do *this* time?' is another. The answers sometimes elicit disbelief and maybe if we are in the right frame of mind,
delight. 'He was in *shul*' – in our local synagogue. 'In *shul*?' – I returned.
The preceding week, my wife had spoken to Shmuel about spending a
Shabbos afternoon with his father – with 'Abba' – in synagogue. But
losing his patience, Shmuel had found his own way.

The sages say: 'On the path that a person sets out, they will take him.'
At first glance, the formulation is confusing, cryptic: should not the
sages have said 'He' as in God 'will take him'? That God will help a
person to continue on that path upon which he has already set out
makes sense. But 'they'? Speculating on the strange plural, Maharsha
offers a seemingly mystical explanation: each of man's thoughts and
deeds creates a *malakh*, or an angel. He who shows a desire to set out
on a good path has angels created from his desires; those angels accompany him on the path upon which he started. When one of my girls
woke up early after resolving to do so the previous night, I greeted her
with a description of legions of angels hovering over her bed, following her down the hallway to wash her hands, and through her morning
routine until she left the house. An imaginative spectacle: in a big
household, she commented, 'You would have a crowd of angels.'

Newsweek ran a cover story years ago asking, 'Do you believe in
angels?' – reporting that the majority of Americans, in fact, do. But, do
we? We are rationalists, and a hallway crammed with angels may be
amusing to a ten-year-old, but it strains the imagination of the skeptical adult. The Jewish tradition, however, is full of angels – from
Abraham welcoming angels into his home in Genesis to the singing of
Shalom Aleihem on Friday nights, welcoming angels to the *Shabbos*
table. Such images, at a remove from the pop-culture idea, may prompt
rethinking about how natural and supernatural relate. When God creates angels from our good initiatives, He gives strength to our resolve
to do good deeds, so that our thoughts, made sure by the help of the
divine, habituate us on the path to further good. Our angels, our good
thoughts, pave the way for us. They are the way God transforms our
first impulses into something more durable and permanent.

Sometimes I succumb to the temptation to think of Shmuel as the exceptional child, different from his 'normal' peers and siblings, wandering without direction. But I learned that afternoon that angels accompany Shmuel as well, that is, even the child who many – even in a culture that only plays lip-service to 'difference' – may consider as forever lost. For on *Shabbos* afternoon, Shmuel's thoughts, the angels that he had inherited had directed him to our synagogue. True, those 'angels' – the thoughts which are the product of our care – may accompany our children to unexpected places. But sometimes, they take them, like Shmuel on that late Saturday afternoon, to just the place we want them to be, first to me in *shul*, and then, in the end, back home.

22 The poetry of the world: God's place

My kids sing at the *Shabbos* table, or when they are painting, or when they want to be adorable, or a nuisance: '*Hashem* is here, *Hashem* is there, *Hashem* is everywhere!' I mostly enjoy it, though when my precocious five-year-old asks with a glint in his eyes, – is 'God in the house? In my remote-control car? In my fingernail,' I pause, and my thoughts turn to Ralph Cudworth.

Ralph who?

Ralph Cudworth – he and some of his mid-seventeenth-century contemporaries became known as 'Cambridge Platonists.' The Cambridge Platonists, sometimes included in histories of Western philosophy, are more often ignored. Cudworth lived in two worlds, or at least so he tried. One, the world of the poets, where physical and spiritual were connected; the other, philosophical, modern, and rationalist, where spirit and matter were forever sundered, distinct, and separate. Cudworth's earlier contemporary, the poet John Milton imagined a world in which Adam and Eve, even after their fall, might see 'Presence Divine,' while Hobbes, the figure at the beginnings of the modern age, saw only the motions of 'artificial limbs.' That God is involved in the universe for Hobbes – as for his predecessor Francis Bacon – was just the 'clouds and fancy' of the poet's 'imagination.'

Cudworth may have loved the older poets, but he was born in the age of philosophers. When Descartes first published his works, Henry More, Cudworth's contemporary, found reason to be cheered: maybe the Frenchman's work would help allow God's continued presence in the universe. But the love affair with Descartes was short-lived, and both Platonists found themselves realizing that he might be as bad as Hobbes – that the two of them together were creating, or even worse, discovering, a universe without God. Richard Dawkins, a contemporary scientist and would-be philosopher gives a modern voice to this view of the world. Life is not Hobbes's 'artificial limbs,' but 'just bytes and bytes and bytes of digital information.' Science does not have to take poetry out of the world, but Dawkins's version of science, notwithstanding his protests, does a pretty good job. There is 'no spirit-driven life force,' Dawkins continues, 'no throbbing, heaving, pollulating, protoplasmic, mystic jelly.' After the philosophers of the seventeenth century, there is either a world of 'bytes of digital information' or in Dawkins condescending take – 'pollulating'? – God fully immersed in the Creation. Accepting the philosophical world-view of the philosophers – and this is where Cudworth was made to feel anxious, because he did – means either one of two things: a world without God, or a world 'heaving' with divinity.

For more than eight hundred pages, Cudworth's ambitiously titled *True Intellectual System of the Universe* gives an obsessive catalog of the heresies of his day, fitting them into one of two categories: those asserting 'a Dead and wooden world' and those asserting – Cudworth cannot decide which is worse – that God is 'everywhere' present, antic-ipating my five-year-old, 'in a Gnat and Fly, Insect and Mite.' In one world, God is absent; in the other, God is merged into His Creation. Cudworth sees a world either empty of God, or so full of the divine as to threaten to make Him totally irrelevant. For who needs God if I can claim the world is divine or that I am myself divine?

Cudworth shows himself nervous about the 'dead wood' belief in a world of only things that would go from Hobbes to Marx to Dawkins's bytes of digitized storage. But he is equally anxious about another modernism that goes from Spinoza and eighteenth-century pantheists to the English Romantic poets to the final vulgar version, Dawkins's opposite number, Shirley MacLaine, shouting out on the beach at East Hampton, 'I am God!' Cudworth, the reluctant philosopher, would have been happier, probably, in the world of the poets, before modern philosophers and their infuriating and irreconcilable oppositions.

But there is a kind of philosophy that, as Wittgenstein writes, should only be written as a form of poetry. The sages confront the problems faced by modern philosophers, but in the language of poetry, midrash. In Genesis, as Jacob leaves Be'er Sheva, 'he happens upon the place,' which Rashi explains to be Mount Moriah, the future site of the Holy Temple in Jerusalem, where the divine presence rests. On this same verse, the sages say, 'God is the place of the world, but the world is not the place of God.' *Ha-Makom* or 'The Place' is a way – they know this from Jacob's chance encounter – of naming God. For the 'place' of the world provides the first intuition of God's presence. We may refer to God as the Place, *Ha-Makom*, as we do in reading the Passover *Hagada*, but the name is *not* one of the holy names of God. To make it so might mislead some to say that the world is the place of God. But God and the world are not identical.

In prayer, the paradox – that God is part of the world and separate from it – also expresses itself. Worshipers, in the call and response at the center of morning and afternoon prayers – the *kedusha* – in imitation of the angels call out to one another, '*Kadosh, Kadosh, Kadosh*' – 'Holy, Holy, Holy is the Lord of Hosts who fills the whole world with His Glory.' And then, following the model of the angelic hosts, 'Blessed is the Glory of God from His Place.' The angels first see a world filled with God's '*Kavod*' or 'Glory.' Nietzsche dreaded what he called the 'weightlessness of things' which he foresaw as a consequence of his own pronouncement of the 'Death of God.' In the call and response of prayer, God's 'glory' – his '*Kavod*' which literally means weightiness or substance – anchors God's presence in the world, giving the world weight. But what follows comes like a retraction, as the angels reply: 'Blessed is the Glory of God from '*His* Place' – '*Mimkomo*.' Maimonides describes this place as God's otherworldly – His distinct and distinguished Place. But the *Makom* which Maimonides describes as 'His Place' has other resonances, more literally and simply the place of the world. So God is at once blessed from His Place, but also from the place of the world. It might make a philosopher's head spin.

But even more: after the angels assert God's presence in the world in the version of the angelic interchange from the Sabbath prayers – 'His Glory fills the world' – they then cry out, now in seeming bewilderment: 'Where is the place of His Glory?' In another version of the angelic exchange, they stand at the foot of God's 'Throne of Glory' yet still ask, 'Where is the place of his Glory?' The Throne of Glory is the way the sages imagine God's otherworldly Glory coming down to earth. But the angels, flying back and forth passing God's Throne still ask: 'Where is He?' God is present, blessed from his Place, but he is also, at the very same time, in his own Place, utterly unknowable, invisible. The angelic call and response ends as the place and space yield to time: 'God will reign forever and ever.' First He is present in the world and then, utterly separate, God vanishes into the infinity of time.

Philosophers may see contradictions, but poets – prayer is also a form of poetry – see, even cultivate, paradox. Not because poets are flighty and fanciful and not interested in the truth, or, as Dawkins frets, 'reason.' But because paradox is a way of apprehending the complexity of a world that cannot be rendered in philosophical categories, certainly not reducible to Dawkins's bytes of information.

'Conflict requires incompatibilities,' Adam Phillips writes of the psyche, and also creates, it should be added, incompatible ways of seeing. We should rather speak of 'paradoxes and spectrums, not contradictions and mutual exclusions.' As Hamlet tells Horatio, 'There are more things in heaven and earth then are dreamt of in your philosophy.' Scientists do not render the world less beautiful, as Dawkins insists religious people claim. Though assuredly some scientists, with their fussy aversion to paradox, do render the world less so.

'Voice is always in the plural,' Phillips also writes. God creates a universe in which we can develop, as poets or scientists, our plural voices. So when my five-year-old asks about the God residing in his fire truck, I tell him, 'God is up in the sky,' not to correct him, but to revise the simplicity of his first take. Because it is never too early to get a taste for paradox, or the poetry of the world.

23 Open minded Torah II: Judaism and postmodernism

Someone called me a postmodernist today. James Kugel, the noted Biblical scholar, standing up for reading 'scientifically' and 'without presuppositions,' says that my way of reading may work for Miltonists (who just happen to be a pretty serious bunch) but not for readers of the Bible – and this is not the first time. Years ago, a physicist, chastised me for writing like a 'post-modernist philosopher' and for not believing in 'objective reality.' Kugel argues that I do not know what the Bible is really about; while this scientist from Haifa maintains that I do not understand Reality.

Social scientists and 'hard' scientists love to dismiss literary critics like me. Scientists are at the top of the totem pole of disciplines – with literary critics and philosophers way down at the bottom. Stephen Weinberg, a Nobel Prize winner in physics, recalls, or so he tells it, that one of his colleagues, 'in facing death,' drew 'some consolation' from the reflection 'that he would never again have to look up the word hermeneutics in the dictionary.' The physicist jests; both Weinberg and his friend know that hermeneutics comes from the Greek word for interpretation. In relating the story, the physicist mocks those like me who say that interpretation is always important. For Weinberg, some people merely interpret, while scientists like himself – *Dreams of a Final Theory* is a coming attraction for a 'final theory' which will account for Everything – just tell the Truth about reality.

If literary critics are toward the bottom of the hierarchy, religious people, for Weinberg, do not even make the list. One of the 'great achievements of science,' Weinberg writes, 'has been, if not to make it impossible for intelligent people to be religious, then at least make it possible for them *not* to be religious.' The fantasy of a world without interpretation, ruled over by updated scientific versions of Plato's philosopher-kings, is also a world with fewer religious people. So Weinberg, wielding 'objective reality,' dismisses literary critics, philosophers, and the religiously-inclined, as overinterpreting, hopelessly subjective postmodernists. Those answering back to Weinberg – and regrettably there are many postmodernists who oblige – 'It's all subjective' or 'Everything is relative' – justify the physicist's sometimes smug conclusions.

But Weinberg's disdain for both interpretation and religion comes in marked contrast to an earlier Nobel Prize winner in physics, A.S. Eddington, who wrote in 1929 that with the quantum revolution in physics, 'it became possible for an intellectual to become religious.' A contemporary of Eddington, Niels Bohr, also at the vanguard of the quantum revolution, performed experiments which had the effect of showing that interpretation – the models which scientists use – effect what they observe. In the set of experiments upon which his 'Copenhagen interpretation' is based, Bohr demonstrates that, depending upon the experiment, light behaves either like a 'wave' or like a 'particle,' but never both at the same time. Like the philosopher's 'duck-rabbit,' one can see, at any one time, only one or the other – duck or rabbit, light or particle.

Describing Bohr's legacy, another Nobel Prize winner in physics, Louis de Broglie, writes, that 'to describe the complexity of reality, it may be necessary to use two, or even more descriptions for a single entity.' 'Now I see it as a duck.' 'Now I see it as a rabbit.' But, those who conclude from Bohr's theory that everything is *only* subjective – and again there is no shortage of postmodernists in the academy who do – go too far. For 'reality,' though it has no perspective of its own, puts constraints upon how it can be perceived. There is no elephant in the picture; and light is not a vector.

The sages say, 'Any dispute which is for the sake of Heaven will endure' – the model for which is the dispute between the Houses of Hillel and Shammai. The two sages argue against one another, even contradict one other: one says 'kosher'; the other, 'not kosher.' But since there is no 'God's eye view' to inhabit – we do not know the mind of God – we need both of them to give voice to the complexity of Torah: 'these and these are the words of the Living God.' The Houses of Hillel and Shammai are 'beloved by God' since it is through them – their interpretations of the Torah given at Sinai – that Torah comes into the world. God does not want such disputes to come to an end; they endure because through them, His Torah is revealed.

What would happen, Hilary Putnam asks, imagining a 'thought experiment,' if God were asked the equivalent of 'Is light a wave or a particle?' God replies, in the scene which the philosopher imagines: 'I don't know.' Putnam does not question God's omniscience. In fact, God's response in Putnam's quantum midrash is similar to the divine response in the dispute over the ritual purity of the oven. After hearing that the sages rejected the miracles performed on behalf of Rabbi Eliezer, Rabbi Nathan meets Elijah the prophet, and asks: 'What did God say at the moment?' The prophet responds: 'He laughed and said, my children have defeated me.' God does not lack knowledge; as the Maharal writes, he encompasses all perspectives. But when the truth of Torah or of quantum reality comes into the world with interpretation – is light a wave or a particle? is the food kosher or not? – then the divine perspective becomes irrelevant. The principles of the sages come together: 'The Torah is not in Heaven'; 'these and these are the words of the Living God.' Torah, like quantum reality, is too complex to be encompassed by a single point of view.

'Seventy *panim* of Torah' – seventy 'faces' of Torah – means not only that the Torah has many 'aspects' or 'sides,' as the phrase is often translated, but that Torah comes into the world as a face, the human face. Putnam's *Reality with a Human Face* challenges philosophers and scientists who see 'objective reality' or 'truth' and the human face as unrelated opposites. 'Torah with a Human Face,' however, is a redundant phrase. For Torah only comes into the world *with* the human face, or with the faces that reveal the many facets or faces – *panim* – of Torah. The sages say that one who sees six hundred thousand Jews, the number of those present at Mount Sinai, or a sage who can fathom the wisdom of the same number, recites a special blessing, 'Blessed is God, the Wise One who knows all secrets.' This sage emulates the divine in knowing the 'wisdom of the faces' – 'Just as every face is different, so their knowledge is different.' This is the secret at the heart of the mystical teachings of the kabbalists: God gives the Torah; the people of Israel receive the Torah. Only in the multitude of human faces are the secrets of Torah revealed.

Stressing the role of interpretation does not mean, if you are a physicist abandoning belief in Reality, or a Jew abandoning belief in Torah. But since we do not live in the mind of God, we have to settle for our own always partial and incomplete – never to be final – understandings of His revelation. So learning Torah does not take place in a quiet library, but in the noisy House of Study. 'When a person is alone, he does not receive the Torah,' the sages say, but only when he brings out more than one aspect, more than one face of the Torah. This is not, however, to be confused with a postmodern pluralism where everything and anything goes, 'It's all subjective.' Learning with a study partner enacts a special kind of knowledge, of knowing through not knowing, or of not-knowing, as knowing. Even as I know – and I see one side of the Torah clearly, so I say, 'Now I see it as a rabbit,' I understand that what I know is just one aspect, partial and incomplete. I do not despair of such knowledge, nor do I celebrate having complete knowledge, the Real Thing, whether it is the Real Bible or the Final Theory.

When the Houses of Hillel and Shammai disagree, the law, in practice, follows the former for they live out the principle of 'the laws of perspective,' that truth is revealed through bringing out its many faces. For the House of Hillel, even in their disagreement, study the teachings of the House of Shammai. Not only that, they mention them first. Not because they are postmodernists before their time, secretly acknowledging that there really is no truth. To the contrary, they believe in their own interpretations so strongly that they must remind themselves: 'Our teaching does not fully define the Torah'; 'There is more to Torah than any single perspective can provide, even our own.'

Hillel himself says, 'If I am not for myself, who will be for me?' The Torah which will help me reveal my face is mine to find. My soul is my own; no one will nurture it for me. 'If I am only for myself,' however, Hillel continues, 'then what am I?' If I am only interested in my Torah, and not the Torah that appears in the face of others, I show my indif-ference to them, but also to the Torah that has many faces. Though *not* a postmodernist before his time, Hillel understood – and his students followed his lead – that the Torah only comes down to earth in the human face.

24 Stepping up

When the people of Israel need a new leader, God turns to Moses: 'Take Joshua ben Nun.' There are different kinds of taking: the word for 'take,' *kakh*, does not only denote a physical action, but, as Rashi explains, the 'taking' is with and through words. No taking-in or forceful recruitment here, but Moses trying to persuade Joshua rationally. It is a lesson for spouses, parents and teachers – to effect change not through force, but with language. Force habituates more force. If you drag an unruly five-year-old to the bath tonight, be prepared to expend equal, or maybe even more energy, tomorrow. Best also not to start with the language of 'you had better,' but with a version of Moses' persuasive words.

It is easy to imagine why Joshua did not want the leadership thrust upon him. 'I am sitting in the House of Study and learning Torah; leave me alone!' So Moses 'takes' his reluctant charge to task by convincing him to accept the mantle of leadership. In the Book of Jeremiah, a similar conversation takes place, this time between God and the author of the work that bears his name: 'I formed you in the womb, I knew you, and before you came forth out of the womb, I sanctified you.' To which Jeremiah, the reluctant prophet-to-be responds: In the womb? Nothing doing; I am still 'young,' a mere child. Find someone else. But God responds in turn: don't tell me about your 'youth'; it's time to step up.

Pinhas, in whom the priesthood will rest, provides the counter image to Joshua and Jeremiah. He is also youthful. But the generation of the desert has reached a crossroads. Bilaam, the prophet of the nations, was unable to curse Israel despite his efforts. Balak, the leader of the Midianites has one last remaining strategy to defeat Israel: to seduce them with the women of his own nation, including his own daughter. In the story in which Pinhas intervenes, Zimri, the Jewish prince of the tribe of Simeon, and Cozbi, the Midianite princess, publically flaunt the divine command, and 'in the eyes of Moses and the people of Israel' – out in the open – commit their brazen act. In the reading of the hasidic master from Izhbits, Zimri is not only a prince, but he is a *tzaddik*, a righteous person. But Zimri is overwhelmed and enveloped by desire for the Midianite princess Cuzbi, and loses himself. He may be righteous, and he may have tried to guard himself from temptation, but, in the end, he succumbs. Through a magnetic attraction which he mistakes for love, Zimri gives in to a desire so strong it affects his ability to see and think. He has the legal status of one under duress, or in more contemporary terms – perhaps the Izhbitser would agree – he is subject to psychic energies he cannot master, that instead master him. Zimri thinks Cozbi is his destined beloved, his *beschert*, but in actuality she activates a lustful desire which he cannot withstand. He hears the soundtrack from *Love Story*, but there is a different kind of music playing.

In the face of the surreal events in the desert, even Moses is unable to act. Zimri taunts him: 'Were you not also involved with a foreign woman? Isn't Tzippora, your wife, also a Midianite?' He continues, 'Was she permissible to you or forbidden?' – the further barb implying, 'Spare me, Moses, your hypocrisy.' When the people of Israel do look to their leader for guidance, he is forgetful. The giver of the Torah does not know the law. From a strictly legal standpoint, Moses is guiltless of the charge Zimri alleges: the prohibition on relations with Midianites comes with the giving of the Torah and Moses marries Tzippora before Mount Sinai. Yet Moses feels some ambivalence, implicated by Zimri's act. Whatever pangs make Moses silent and forgetful – there must be something to Zimri's claim – the people of Israel are left abandoned to tears, overwhelmed by a mixture of desire, guilt, and fear.

In the midst of all this, the youthful Pinhas approaches Moses and says, 'Don't you see what's happening before your eyes?' He continues, 'You yourself taught me the law about Midianite women.' To which Moses responds, using a set of metaphors which again suggests that he is trying to distance himself: 'You received the letter, now be its executioner.' The man who came down Mount Sinai to confront a rebellious nation of thousands is silent, caught up in the turbulence of his own feelings. So the people of Israel weep at the entrances of their tents. When the prince is suffering from a fatal attraction, the whole generation is dysfunctional and even the leader is unable to act – though he does have the presence of mind to delegate – Pinhas sees, and acts. The verse in Numbers says that Pinhas 'stood up from within the assembly,' so the Psalmist says of him, 'he stood up and intervened.'

Though not called upon by God in this direct fashion, sometimes we have a sense of a mission that calls us, we feel the need to step up. But like the prophets, we find reasons to avoid action. And they are always good reasons, or seem to be. 'I'm not ready.' 'I'm too young.' Or there are other kinds of avoidance, of these there are never a shortage: apathy, depression, fear. The poet John Milton felt washed up at twenty-three, verging on despair, and giving up: 'My late spring,' the poet laments, 'no bud or blossom shew'th.' But feeling belated, as Milton does, or too young, are equivalent ways of what T.S. Eliot calls 'cheering oneself up,' really just subconsciously justifying inactivity, and escaping the demands of reality.

'There must be someone else' – the youthful prophets protest. To Joshua and Jeremiah, God says: 'There are certainly ambitious men who will step into your shoes, but I want you.' We are not prophets, but sometimes the clarity of a vision – for change, for *tikkun*, for rectifying the world – may call. We will not likely be called upon by our nation, yet we may be by our families, our schools, our workplaces by a vision which no one else sees, or others are dissuaded from seeing, simply too afraid to confront. So when those around us are under duress because of fear or guilt or whatever, we should not give in to the weaker part of ourselves, or to other more ambitious men and politicians. Sometimes, we have to step up.

25 Prayer and the people: A new *siddur*

My first prayer book – one that I really studied and knew – was not a Jewish *siddur*, but the Book of Common Prayer, first published under King Edward VI in England in 1549. Like many Jews studying English literature, I knew much more about Christianity than Judaism, certainly more about Christian prayer than the Jewish *siddur*. So I knew that by the time Charles I was King of England in the mid-seventeenth century, the Book of Common Prayer was *the* prayer book of the English nation. But the poet of *Paradise Lost*, John Milton, rejects all organized prayer. Prayer must be 'voluntary,' Milton writes: 'He who prays must consult first with his heart.'

In graduate school, I often wondered: what if there was a religion which combined Milton's Puritan commitment to the authenticity of the individual voice and Catholicism's emphasis on tradition and ritual? Though I did not realize, even after years of Sunday school, afternoon Hebrew school classes on Tuesdays and Thursdays and a Bar Mitzva, that the religion for which I was searching in the seminar rooms overlooking Amsterdam Avenue was my own. When a new Jewish prayer book recently came out – the Reform Movement's *Mishkan T'filah* – claiming to be both traditional and innovative, I was interested.

The first reform prayer book – definitely not a *siddur* – but the *Union Prayer Book* was published in 1895. Those who put it together saw Judaism as representing a 'spirit of broad humanity,' a 'progressive religion ever striving to be in accord with the postulates of reason.' In this new rational (and very respectable) brand of Judaism, there were 'ministers,' not rabbis, and a prayer service that removed any signs of Jewish chosenness. There is no mention of Temple worship, redemption, the messianic age, or the return to the Land of Israel. The prayer book took the Jews out of the ghetto, in the process taking away any special claims for Judaism. Moving away from universalism to the diversity of the post-sixties generation, the next Reform prayer book,

Gates of Prayer of 1975, opened to all voices, or rather all movements and ideologies with ten Sabbath evening services, including one 'humanistic' service without any mention of God.

The *Union Prayer Book*, as a Reform rabbi Elliot Stevens observes, suppresses the 'cacophony' of the prayer or '*davening*' of Eastern European Jews; *Gates of Prayer* brought back the noise in social terms, though, as Reform rabbis admit, in the process threatened the unity of the movement. 'If we are all things,' says Lawrence Hoffman, a professor of Hebrew Union College, 'we are nothing.' The new '*siddur*' – a departure even in name – now appears after two decades of preparation, including grants, a blind competition for editorial direction, discussions groups, and field studies. All of this makes what Hoffman terms 'the people's prayer book,' attempting to balance the excesses of its predecessors, the *Union Prayer Book*'s emphasis on the universal and *Gates of Prayer*'s emphasis on diversity.

Rather than do away with the particularity, as in the somber and detached *Union Prayer Book*, or risk a diversity out of control as in *Gates of Prayer*, the layout of the new *siddur* aspires to express difference while framing and containing it – a Reform attempt at Dr. Johnson's '*discordia concors*,' or a discordant harmony. The right-facing pages offer Hebrew texts, transliterations, and conventional English translations; the left-facing page frames free translations, meditations and literary works, including poems by authors ranging from the medieval Ibn Gabirol to Adrienne Rich and Delmore Schwartz. But the attempt to unite differences turns into what Johnson says the poetry of John Donne – 'the most heterogeneous ideas yoked by violence together' – too many different and competing works and perspectives 'yoked' uncomfortably together in one prayer book.

And there is more: beneath the main translations, there are 'spiritual commentaries.' After a shortened extract from the *Shema* comes a meditative translation, flanked beneath by commentaries from the sages of the Talmud and Martin Buber. The sage Abaye elicits the connection between study of Torah and ethics; Buber is cited as advocating an ethics 'as if there were no God.' To further multiply the available perspectives, the 'stage directions' give even more options, 'for those who choose' to add the word '*emet*' ('it is true') as an affirmation of the Biblical passage which precedes. So – and here is where the problems of the prayer book really begin – one either affirms the belief in the one God who took the people out of Egypt, or ... not?

The ever-present 'for those who choose' in *Mishkan T'filah* shows the emphasis on performance and choice. 'Performance of prayer matters more than fixed words,' the *siddur* editor Elyse Frishman asserts, and so prayer leaders are instructed to choose only one prayer per 'page spread,' making for a spontaneous and 'integrated' service. But the choices are sometimes dizzying. Four versions, for example, of *Aleinu*, the traditional prayer that ends services are included, showing different attitudes toward the nations and the special place of Israel (again, or not) among them, as well as versions of prayers which either do or do not mention the resurrection of the dead. Does one make a split-second evaluation of belief in the eternality of body and soul?

Amidst the innovation, there is nostalgia as well, as the *siddur* editor imagines Reform congregations becoming like those 'vital congregations' of the past who knew 'their order of worship and moved through it with deep familiarity.' Generations of Jews have integrated the cadences of David's Psalms into their lives. But how likely is it that congregants commit to memory David Meltzer's 'Tell them I'm struggling to sing with angels . . . . Tell them I sit here invisible in space; nose running, coffee cold & bitter'? Reading Yehuda Amichai's 'The Diameter of the Bomb' as a meditation on the traditional prayer for peace may lead to admiration of the verse, and perhaps the editor's ingenuity, but not to cultivating a personal voice in prayer. The question that keeps coming to mind when turning the pages of *Mishkan T'filah* is: what happened to the 'I' in all of this?

The irony of the new Reform *siddur* is that with all of the distance traveled from the *Union Prayer Book*, the current prayer book remains clergy-centered. Frishman explains to worshipers that 'prayer must move us beyond ourselves.' 'Prayer should not reflect "me,"' she continues, but rather should 'reflect *our* values and ideals.' For all of the emphasis in the volume on the ideal that 'many voices' be spontaneously heard, in the end, the voices are already pre-packaged and supplied, the 'me' lost. *Mishkan T'filah* emphasizes an *ideal* of social diversity, but enforced from the top down. One should not, Frishman warns, look to pages of the *siddur* to 'find one's particular voice.' The prayer book instead is the voice of the movement. But the movement, like its new prayer book, seems without a center, splintering into a postmodern collection of disparate beliefs, unified only by a top-down imposition of the 'values' of 'Reform Judaism and Life.' This is the Reform version of 'the most heterogeneous ideas,' yoked together by the abstract belief in 'social justice, feminism, Zionism, distinctiveness, human challenges.'

Frishman writes that it is 'critical that Reform Jews know what's expected of them.' 'You gotta serve somebody,' Dylan sings, and Frishman wants to make sure that those using *Mishkan T'filah* serve the right ideals. But what remains unclear is whether contemporary worshipers will heed a clergy enjoining them to pursue what is expected, to hold back the energies of difference (not to mention assimilation) and to pursue the 'higher value of community.' In *Mishkan T'filah*, the abstract concept of '*our* values and ideals' takes precedence over the individual. For this new prayer book celebrates 'peoplehood,' but not the individual voices of the people.

Jonathan Sacks, editor of a traditional *siddur* acknowledges a different model for prayer in which the 'order' and 'structures' of the prayers, set down by the Men of the Great Assembly two thousand years ago, allow for refining the individual voice in prayer. Milton – the great iconoclast and rejecter of set-forms – also knew as much. Even as he called for spontaneous prayer, *his* Adam and Eve, when they pray in *Paradise Lost,* borrow the forms of David's Psalms. A voice matures not by rejecting traditional forms, but by embracing them, making them personal. But *Mishkan T'filah* does not take that risk, and so provides the voices ready-made, instead of cultivating them, and thus may fail to build a community united in authentic worship. For all of its idealism, the new *siddur* expends little effort eliciting what King David calls 'prayer from the depths' – the stirrings of the individual soul, expressing itself through the accrued resonances of centuries old prayers, striving towards the divine.

26 A religion for adults?

One Friday night in synagogue, the rabbi spoke of a businessman in Baltimore who returned to the ways of his forefathers in his latter years. Though not able to learn Torah like many of his newfound peers who excelled in the House of Study, he did find other ways to express his commitment to Torah and Jewish life, among them *tzedaka*, or charity, and good deeds. For himself and his wife, *tzedaka* was a personal affair, becoming what Rabbi Joseph Soloveitchik describes as a 'worshipful performance,' an expression of their heartfelt devotion in the service of God.

But then came the financial crisis, the tumble of the NASDAQ, the fall of Lehman, the bailout, and the story of widespread failure and economic hardship. Their portfolio declined forty-five percent; profits diminished, while expenses were rising. The couple hoped to continue giving *tzedaka* as they had in previous years, though in their current circumstances, by springtime, they had already depleted their funds, fulfilling as many of their obligations for charity as they were able. The business man's wife, not wanting to disappoint the expectations of those to whom they had given years before, in an act of selflessness, declared herself willing to give up her split-level suburban home for a modest apartment. The husband was not so sure, but was prevailed upon to consult a well-known sage in B'nai Brak in Israel about their predicament. Of course, the businessman, now sorely down on his luck, had fulfilled his charitable obligations. But the rabbi told him that if he and his wife nevertheless found causes that they deemed worthy, they should persevere and continue to give, even if it meant moving house. The wife was delighted, he less so, but taking the advice of the sage, they determined to change their way of life to give as they had in previous years.

An inspirational story, though it continues.

A few days pass, their re-dedication still high upon their hearts, when the businessman received a phone call from his Swiss equities broker who managed a large portion of his investments. An error had been made; holdings had not been properly cataloged; account statements not properly calculated. Wonderful to relate, his account showed a surplus in the range of several million dollars. Not only did this cover previous losses, but the newly found income made the couple wealthier than ever before. No need to sell the grand piano; the couple stayed put.

A triumphant glance radiates from the rabbi relating the story; satisfied smiles and audible sighs of praise emerge all round. But when the warm feelings dissipate, I remember another story – of the Patriarch Abraham, his brother Haran, and the wicked tyrant Nimrod. The sages say that when Terakh discovered his son's belief in the one God, he promptly turned him over to King Nimrod, who threw him in a fiery furnace: 'If your God is indeed all powerful,' Nimrod boasts to Abraham, 'let Him rescue you.' Meanwhile, on the sidelines, Haran calculates – 'If Abraham is killed, then I am all for Nimrod; if, however, by some chance he survives, I am with Abraham.' When Abraham emerges, miraculously unscathed, Nimrod asks Haran, 'And whose side are you on?' True to himself, Haran answers, 'I am for Abraham.' And Nimrod throws Haran into the furnace.

Haran makes his calculations not on principle, but on cost-benefit. He does not consult the mandates of his faith, but rather his desire for material compensation. 'If Abraham turns out to be father of all the nations of the world, I will be his right-hand man ... and if not,' thinking like a politician, 'I will find something to do in Nimrod's government.'

The message of the story told about the businessman from Baltimore is similar (as different and noble as *his* intentions had been): do a good deed, and receive compensation. All of this is as if to say to God: 'Let's be business partners. I will do my share of the *mitzvot*; you protect my family from hardship. If you can throw in some earthly reward, that will be fine as well. But, whatever I give to you the Almighty, I will expect the dividends.' This may be what some religious people believe, but it is what Rabbi Joseph Soloveitchik calls the mentality of a 'religion for children' – the pragmatic *quid pro quo*, the calculation and anticipated receipt of just returns. This is not only childish, but dangerous. For what happens when God is not the business partner I expect? Do I break off the business arrangement? After all, childish expectations yield to childish disappointment. The facile stories of simple reward – we do not know the nature of the reward for any given *mitzva* – may lead to not just disappointment, but despair. 'This business arrangement,' I may come to think, 'is not working out the way I had anticipated.' And then what?

The couple from Baltimore did the right thing. But with the coda of wealth and reward, it becomes part of a canon of children's literature with the predictable and mandatory happy endings. Though we may hope for such endings, our 'end' in the moment in which we live, as Maimonides writes, is to refine our thinking and ennoble our actions. So the story of the businessman from Baltimore, without the guaranteed happy ending, fits in a different and more demanding canon of stories, that of a complex religion, or more simply a religion for adults.

The purveyors of happy endings – and in our post-holocaust generation there is, strangely, a near-cultural obsession with them – assume there are no longer any adults in the audience. But I am betting otherwise.

Hang around pulpit rabbis long enough and you know it is summer time when talk starts about having to work on sermons for the Days of Awe or High Holidays. 'The congregants only remember two things,' Rabbi Harvey Belovski of Golders Green joked to me on a recent visit to London, 'the length of the *tekia gedola*,' the long last *shofar* blast at the end of the additional service on *Rosh Ha-shana* and 'the rabbi's jokes.' So in late June, he had already begun, he told me, working on his jokes for September. Of course, in some sense, he was joking – but about a serious matter.

The ability to joke – a sense of humor and irony – may be just what the leaders of our generation require, and what some of them lack. Recounting Freud's last days in the Vienna of the late 1930s, Mark Edmundson writes of the model of the leader without a sense of humor, the fascist dictator who sees what he wants and takes it, without qualms or second thoughts. Monolithic and humorless, without doubts, he has no inner conflicts or complexity. Or rather, he may have them, but he *represses* them, and presents himself as without ambivalence or doubts. But 'ambivalence,' as Jeffrey Perl writes, 'is an achievement.'

For Freud, surprisingly, the foil to the fascist dictator is Moses, the figure who even in Freud's idiosyncratic and ambivalent rendering of his life and times, emerges as the ideal leader. In Freud's reading, Moses is the 'hero of sublimation,' achieving his authority not by being 'self-willed and appetitive,' but by 'rechanneling his human impulses and teaching others to do the same.' For Freud, this personality, the ideal but human leader, is not averse to making a joke. Jokes, as Edmundson writes, 'show awareness that there is more than one simple reality to take into account,' testifying to there being 'contending forces at play in the world, contending interpretations of experience.' Genuine leaders are complex because of an appreciation of the complexity of the world reflected in their own psyches. Such leaders, it often turns out, know how to tell a good joke.

Korah, we have seen, is the dictator of the desert, no laughs from him. He fixates on his singular desires and his one truth, the model of the one who engages in dispute for *his* own sake and interest, not for truth or community or God. The Houses of Hillel and Shammai, in contrast to Korah, engage in disputes that reveal a truth that cannot be grasped through a single-minded knowingness. The two may argue, but they acknowledge that they need one another: as Hillel says, 'If I am only for myself, what am I?'

Freud quotes Karl Abel, 'Man is not able to acquire any conceptions otherwise than in contrast with their opposite' – every insight has its parallel opposite insight. Centuries earlier, the Maharal wrote that 'any concept is only known through its opposite.' The understanding shared by the Jews from Prague and Vienna explains the dynamics of the dispute between the sages, how any single perspective shows its inadequacy and hints at that which opposes it. There is no single answer, no perfect interpretation, but rather an equilibrium of inadequate, but nonetheless true, interpretations. The Houses of Hillel and Shammai recognize that to understand God's Creation and revelation, one must nurture an ability to see things from more than one perspective. Korah inhabits a simple monochrome world; Hillel and Shammai one of difference and complexity.

In the sometimes grinding seriousness and defensiveness of contemporary Jewish life, however, even when studying the disputes of Hillel and Shammai and their descendants – who, let's face it, have long known how to tell jokes – we forget the complexity that has defined the Jewish experience since Sinai. Jokes allow for what Jonathan Lear calls 'the sympathetic subversion of a pretense' – a way of undoing the single-mindedness that turns into stridency, or worse. Irony especially is the subtle way of undoing a defense, of opening up a space from which the certainty of one's commitments look different than first thought. Irony does not abolish belief, but allows for a perspective between cynicism and aspiration. It does not demystify all striving, but may reveal what unselfconscious earnestness and enthu-siasm may leave out or repress.

Sometimes only the well-placed joke – told gently enough – can undo unearned certainties. Irony, as Lear writes, is the capacity to real-ize that we may have questions when we thought we had answers. A *talmud hakham*, a Torah scholar, may learn on his own, without a study partner, not because he has all the answers, but because he has internalized the voice – undermining the stridency of singular convic-tions – that always asks questions. He is no longer afraid of them. He will also be the kind of person who can take a joke, who has devel-oped a capacity for irony, that requires, as Freud writes, one to 'hear the opposite' to what he had first thought.

Losing the capacity for irony means becoming more like Korah and Edmundson's fascist personalities of the last century. Trauma should make us wary of a world without irony, but sometimes it makes us more defensive and more susceptible to single-mindedness. We are all, after all, as Freud points out, fundamentalists and fascists, at least potentially. But for Freud, jokes and irony – acknowledging complex-ity and providing a space for both creativity and commitment – are the antidote for such a tendency. Part of the solution, for us, may be finding a rabbi who knows how to tell a joke.

28 Don't take away my *mitzva*!

When a child is born in our neighborhood, offers of help – expressions of care or *hesed* – are fast to follow: volunteers to provide babysitting, housecleaning, and, of course, food, tons of food. So the refrigerator fills up with foil pans of tofu with sesame noodles, chicken *paprikash*, and spaghetti and meatballs. With the birth of our son Shmuel, there was an avalanche, including a month's supply of eggplant parmesan, stored in neat piles in a next-door neighbor's freezer. In gratitude, a few weeks later my wife sent our generous neighbor a gift, a pair of white winter gloves she had bought at the Good Will in Minneapolis the previous summer.

But my daughter Freidie, who had been charged with the delivery, came back with them, the tissue paper in place and the gloves still in the box. Oh, I thought – didn't she want them? There was no card or message, but, then the phone rang, the neighbor on the line: 'Don't take away *my mitzvah*! Please keep the gloves.'

Now, the gloves were not a payment, and I am pretty sure my wife did not offer them in exchange, a gloves-for-eggplant-parmesan deal. There is principle in Proverbs that it is best to avoid taking gifts, but our neighbor's response did not seem to capture the spirit of Solomon's wisdom. When my wife did get home, I handed her the box: 'I guess she didn't like them.'

Rabbi Shimon ben Gamliel says, 'One who finds a child by himself and feeds him, should leave a sign for the parents so they will know that he has eaten.' Not just a practical lesson to prevent obesity in young children – 'your toddler already ate' – but one that leaves a signature of one's goodness so when the mother returns, she will ask her child, 'Did someone come say hello while I was gone?' The child will respond, 'Yes, your friend was here and she gave me a rice cake as well.' And so, Rashi writes, 'the parents will feel that they are loved, and love will grow among the people of Israel.'

We did feel loved, very much so, with the abundance of food and good will. But the response – we understood that our neighbor did not care to take gifts – gave us some pause. *Mitzvot* are a way of connecting between God and man, but they also connect people. Of all the *mitzvot*, *hesed* focuses most on the latter relationship. But with the emphasis placed on the possessive adjective – '*my mitzva*,' I felt like we were just a pretext – with the eggplant parmesan – for the relationship which was foremost in her mind. 'This is between me and Him, so please don't get in the way.'

Hesed is demanding, not like *tzedaka* or charity. The latter is more easily fulfilled, as the synagogue rabbi explained when we lived in Los Angeles: 'When someone comes to the door, write a check.' Smile, write the check, close the door. But the 'care' – the usual translation 'loving kindness' is inadequate – entailed in *hesed* means first finding out what another lacks. When the Torah in Deuteronomy enjoins showing an open hand to one who lacks, I am being told to give, Rashi writes, according to what a person had been accustomed, even 'a horse and carriage, and a messenger to run in front him.' So when the Wall Street lawyer hits hard times, I must be sensitive to his needs, to see what he now misses, in his case, perhaps, a BMW, a Rolex watch, and a Cisco Conference networking system. Admittedly, Bernie Madoff, or even those who lost their money honestly, may not be high on my *hesed* list. I may have other priorities, but the Torah tells me to be prepared to see what another lacks.

We feel need, and experience lack. But *hesed*, writes Maimonides, shows itself as the excess or enthusiasm that fills the lack experienced by others. This is the excess, Rabbi Joseph Soloveitchik explains, of opening oneself up, making oneself present to another. I need to abandon the barrier – *hesed* may be a risky business – that separates me from others. By nature I am an existential miser – I do not want to give up my inner life – but *hesed* demands that I do so. With *tzedaka*, I open my checkbook, with *hesed*, I open up *myself*. Such care means a willingness to know and see the distress experienced by another person. The *bildungsroman* – the coming of age novel of Moses – is encapsulated in a single verse in Exodus: 'And it came to pass in those days, when Moses was grown, he went out to his brothers, and looked upon their suffering.' The coming of age story for Moses has two parts: first, making himself present to his brothers and then becoming aware of their suffering. Later, Moses, alone in the desert, turns to look upon the burning bush. In the sages' reading, God says: 'You turned away from your own concerns to the sufferings of others, and so I will speak with you.' So in the continuation of the story in Exodus, God calls out to Moses from the bush. The divine presence does not show itself through mystical incantations or as a result of solitary longings, but by the act of seeing the hardships of others.

Hesed and *mishpat*, or care and judgment, come together, says the Psalmist. As Rabbi Joseph Soloveitchik writes, following the kabbalists, *hesed* means the expansion of the self, while *mishpat* or judgment means self-limiting or contraction. I am commanded to extend myself to others, but doing so, Rabbi Soloveitchik writes, depends upon being able to contract myself as well. *Hesed* that turns into a performative religiosity, which is only about me and my dramatic religious persona, is not just a lower form of *hesed*, says Rabbi Soleveitchik, but it is 'a fantasy.' Not care, but egotism. If I do not limit myself, then I do not leave any possibility for others to enter into my world. *Hesed* without the presence of *mishpat* is narcissism. For what announces itself as giving – 'Look, I am doing a *mitzva*!' – becomes an expression of a desire to fill the world with myself. Even God, say the kabbalists, withdraws from the world to leave a space for man.

There are those who are inclined to give of their excess, to show their influence. But *hesed* means being able to receive as well. Without that capacity my giving may just be an expression of selfish desire, a means of dramatizing my power and influence over others, or my supposed connection to God. Opening to the other – and being able to get something back, even something as insignificant as a pair of gloves – may be a sign of what it really means to care.

Springtime in Jerusalem, when my wife and I – yet once more – try to find a school for our son Shmuel with Down syndrome, this time in a *heder*, a pre-K class in our neighborhood.

Earlier in the week, we had set up a meeting with the principal of a school nearby. To our surprise, he was not dismissive, even cordial. Though there had not been a child in his school with Down syndrome for a generation, he seemed open to helping with the education of Shmuel. We were invited back the following day to meet with one of the teachers and an administrator to discuss logistics, how to integrate Shmuel and his 'shadow' into the classroom. We spoke to the prospective teacher as well: 'My business is to teach children; and I will do my best to teach Shmuel, just as I would with any other child.' 'Though I am not a professor,' he continued with a wink, 'I do have thirty years experience.'

As we were leaving – '*s'yata d'shmaya*,' heavenly assistance, my wife said – another teacher, seeing Shmuel tagging along, stopped us to volunteer that he had been a classmate of the boy with Down syndrome years back. To the questions which reflected the principal's primary concerns – 'Will Shmuel be disruptive?'; 'Will he be accepted by the other boys?'; 'Will he want to participate in class? – the teacher offered assurances. As Tolstoy might put it, no two children are alike, and no two children with Down syndrome are alike. But the teacher echoed what we had told the principal: his classmate had been full of joy, eager to participate, not at all disruptive. Shmuel's affability and good cheer – traits which prompt my wife to wonder what I would be like with an extra chromosome – as well as his cognitive high-functioning, we explained, brought us to mainstreaming and this school in the first place.

A few days passed. I left some messages with the school secretary; my calls were not returned. When I did reach the principal, he suggested

I speak to someone else in the school – this the fourth person – who would make the 'final' decision. It did not sound good; instead, I pressed him.

'It's a very difficult decision . . .' His voice trailed off. 'Don't take this the wrong way Rabbi Kolbrener, and please don't be insulted. . . .'

Calling me rabbi, I thought to myself, was a bad sign.

'It's a matter,' he hesitated, 'of considering the *mossad*.' Not just an elementary school, now it was an 'institute.'

'What about the *mossad*?'

'The reputation.'

I was silent.

'We have to think of what other parents will say when they see a child like Shmuel in the class with their normal children. How will we be able to justify it to them? These parents also have to be respected.'

I was not insulted; in fact, I had heard versions of this before. Likely, I thought, that someone from whom he had sought advice had a different view of the 'institute,' and was forcing him – he sounded conflicted – to do what was against his better judgment. So I responded: 'We both know that what you are now advocating – acquiescing to close-mindedness and sanctioning fear of difference – is against our *hashgafa*, our worldview, indeed,' I continued, 'any perspective based on the Torah.' 'It's a *hilul Hashem*,' I went on, 'a desecration of God's name, to send us to schools outside of our community when you acknowledged yourself that Shmuel might have a chance to thrive in one of your classrooms.'

'And as far as "normal" children,' I went on, inflecting the quotation marks around the word 'normal' where he did not, 'we are not children of Esau who find perfection in this world, but children of Israel, of Jacob, who acknowledge that this world is a place of lack and imperfection.' 'I am a pragmatist,' I continued: 'if Shmuel does not integrate into the classroom, we will take him out immediately, but if the experiences of our home, our building and of his nursery school are true, then Shmuel's presence will be a blessing not just for him, but for all who have the chance to be around him.'

'Rabbi Kolbrener' – again the wrong title – 'what you say is all *emet l'emito* – the undeniable truth, *k'dosh k'doshim*, the holy of the holies, but,' and I could see him shrugging his shoulders, 'we live in "*olam ha-sheker*,"' a world of lies. Here it was – the *olam ha-sheker* excuse. I had heard people exclaim '*olam ha-sheker*' as an expression of frustration; this was the first time I heard it as an excuse. Making the *olam ha-sheker* excuse not as a form of consolation, but as justification for doing the wrong thing, makes the Torah something theoretical – 'We can't actually live by the words of Torah.' Torah ceases to be a handbook for *tikkun olam*, the redemption of the world, but an ideal to which we aspire when not in conflict with our prejudices and fears. The principal, to his credit, was honest, acknowledging that my words were true, even holy. But from the *olam ha-sheker* perspective, truth and holiness are abstractions, finding no place in the world. So Judaism transforms into a religion of ideals only. How often is such an excuse, even when left unuttered, used to justify laziness, self-interest or even corruption?

Traditions in the West in literature, philosophy, and theology – from Homer to Plato to the apostle Paul – separate the ideal, take it out of the world. But Judaism, and this was one of the reasons that I started, many years ago, to split my time between the library and the House of Study, transforms the real into the ideal, elevating the world. Judaism offers the promise of a learning which is not only theoretical – like those earnest discussions I used to have in graduate school – but a learning leading to action, *tikkun olam*. Socrates is quoted as saying, 'Man must rise above the earth, to the top of the atmosphere and beyond.' The sages say, 'It is not in Heaven'; the Torah has to be brought down to earth. Even for a little boy with Down syndrome.

'Our loss is unbearable' says the prime minister of Israel on *Yom Ha-Shoah*, Holocaust Remembrance Day. After such loss, how does one go on? The question has been asked, with good reason, for centuries. Mourning, the philosopher Stanley Cavell writes, is the work of a lifetime. But why would anyone want to spend a lifetime learning how to mourn?

The sages say: 'Three thousand laws were forgotten during the period of mourning for Moses.' With Moses' death, laws from the Torah are lost as well. When Moses is alive – he has a special relationship with God – he simply asks, and receives a single and unambiguous answer. As the story continues, the people of Israel, in the face of loss, turn to Joshua, the anointed leader of Israel, and demand: 'Ask.' That is, 'ask God to tell us the laws that were forgotten.' The people of Israel prefer certainty, and they want Joshua to provide it. To their disappointment, Joshua is turned away, as God quotes the verse from Deuteronomy: 'It is not in Heaven.' The Torah was already given at Mount Sinai, and is now in your hands. To the persistent request for divine resolution of doubts – the people of Israel later ask the same of Pinhas, Elazar, and Samuel – God responds each time, 'the Torah is not in Heaven.'

When Freud presents his inventive version of the death of Moses in *Moses and Monotheism*, he emphasizes the Jewish people's guilt for the supposed crime of having killed the giver of the Law. For the sages, it is not guilt with which the people are fraught, but anxiety about living in a world of loss, without the presence of the leader Moses. And they have good reason to be anxious: 'Three thousand laws were forgotten during the period of mourning for Moses.' 'After Moses' death,' the story this time continues, 'if those who declared a vessel to be impure were in the majority, it was deemed impure; and if those declared it pure were in the majority, it was deemed pure.' Moses knew the law.

But for the generations after Moses' death, the law becomes a subject of debate as the people of Israel experience disagreement and doubt.

How to bear up to the loss of Moses' passing? As the sages relate, Joshua does not know. 'When Moses was about to leave this world, he turns to Joshua: "Ask me to resolve any uncertainties you have."' Moses offers to allay the uncertainties and doubts that he knows will follow his death. But the younger prophet, Joshua responds: 'Did I ever for a minute go to another place?'; 'I was always by your side, your right hand-man.' 'At that moment,' the sages say, 'Joshua felt weak; he forgot three hundred laws, and seven hundred doubts entered his mind.' The younger prophet is in denial, not ready to face his teacher's death and the prospect of having to mourn, so part of the tradition that is entrusted to him is lost. At this, the people of Israel are enraged. So much so that they turn on Joshua and try to kill him. Freud says that the people of Israel killed Moses because they did not want the burden of the Law that he was commanded by God to bestow. But the sages say that the Jewish people wanted to kill Joshua for the opposite reason – because he forgot the Law. Facing Joshua's failure to retrieve the Law as it was, they prefer doing away with him, as well as the inheritance for which he now stands. Anxious about not having the Law as it once was – perfect and complete – they want to forget it altogether.

For the people of Israel, it is either all or nothing: they pine for the transcendent and absolute truth represented by Moses: 'We want him back!' and the perfect Torah that he represents. But when they realize that Joshua is unable to carry on the tradition of Moses – they cannot bear the uncertainty – they call for the younger prophet's death. To Hilary Putnam's principle, 'Enough isn't everything, but enough is enough,' the people of Israel, protest loudly, 'We want everything!' They want to be passive recipients of the Truth represented by Moses, or they will have nothing more to do with it.

In the stories of Moses' death, the sages offer a sociology of the Jewish people, then and now. There are those who fixate on the image of the past and fantasize an absolute truth, the continued presence of Moses and a past exactly as it once was; and those, recognizing the impossibility of attaining such Truth, who abandon tradition altogether.

Either the fundamentalism of a belief in an absolute truth, or the postmodern rejection of *any* possibility of truth. Open the pages of the Israeli newspaper *Haaretz* on any day, and you feel like you are back in the Sinai desert in the day of Moses' passing. In anxious denial of uncertainty, the people of Israel continue to argue for absolutes. But maintaining a belief in truth in the face of loss, a truth which is not absolute, means knowing how to mourn: 'A thousand and seven hundred laws were forgotten during the period of mourning for Moses. Rabbi Abbahu said: Nevertheless Otniel, the son of Kenaz, restored them through *pilpul* – his "sharp wit."' Otniel knows how to mourn.

Joshua is the passive middle-man, in denial, lacking the courage to take on the challenge imposed by mourning. Otniel, for the sages, is a better candidate for passing on tradition. He conquers, in the Book of Judges, *Kiryat Sefer*, literally the City of the Book. Moses twice blesses Joshua with courage, a sure sign that the latter, at least in his youth, lacked it. Such courage, what Jonathan Lear calls a primary psychoanalytic virtue, means first facing up to loss. When the 'fabric of life is ripped,' there is the need for courage, to acknowledge loss and death before looking forward. Joshua, like the Israelites who seek divine intervention to make up for their loss, avoids creativity and responsibility. For the sages, Otniel shows courage not just in military battle, but in the more important war, the war of Torah, the conquest of the Book. Yabetz, Otniel's other name, contains the root letters of the word pain: he 'was born of pain.' Otniel's *pilpul* – his sharp-witted engagement – represents a courageous way of owning up to the past, providing a path into the future. Out of the pain and loss transformed through mourning, Torah continues. Otniel does not simply repeat the past, nor does he turn away from it. He is engaged rather in what Freud calls creative memory – the turning back that leads forward.

There are memories, Adam Phillips, writes, which are forms of forgetting. Fixating on the past, clamoring, 'We want Moses back,' may be memory as forgetting. Otniel certainly does not forget Sinai or Moses, but his mourning, what Freud calls a 'partial leave-taking' of the past, allows enough distance from the memory of Moses so that he can remember. There are two kinds of people who cannot mourn: those who are in denial about loss, clinging to their fantasy of a past still present; they are stuck in the past. And there are those who are in denial that there is anything to mourn; they have abandoned the past altogether. They are mirror images of one another, united in a codependency of extremism and denial. Neither understand the paradox that Moses is dead; the Torah of Moses lives on. As Lear writes 'Only when one kills off the messenger, can his message finally be installed.' Only when Moses is acknowledged to be dead can the creative relationship to the Torah begin anew. So creativity begins with the uncertainty that comes from loss.

The insight that creativity and loss come together starts with Moses himself. After the giving of the Ten Commandments and his ascent to the heavens for forty days, Moses comes down the mountain to find the people – according to their mistaken calculations Moses was late – worshipping the golden calf. Moses hurls the tablets to the ground, shattering them at the foot of the mountain. As the sages recount, God praises Moses – '*yashar koah*!' – a job well done! The sages see the giving of the Torah as repairing the sin of the garden of Eden and bestowing immortality and an immutable memory upon the people of Israel: 'If not for the breaking of the first tablets, the Torah would never have been forgotten.' Yet when Moses breaks the tablets, God offers his praise. About this divine praise, the sages say, 'Sometimes the Torah needs to be undone for it to be sustained.' True, the Law cannot be nurtured in a culture of idolatrous worship. But more than that, by smashing the tablets, Moses makes room for memory and the beginnings of tradition in a world of forgetting. 'The gap we make by the act of forgetting,' as Phillips writes, is what allows for creativity.

The many faces of Torah come into being only through forgetting, and the second tablets, are not written by 'the finger of God,' as the first tablets, but by Moses himself. The people of Israel pass from the realm without death and forgetting to the realm of loss in which Moses crafts the tablets, providing a model for man's creativity in the face of forgetting. The first dispute among the sages comes about through forgetting. For such forgetting, and the creative remembrance it ideally nurtures, leads to the difference of perspective – 'these and these' – of which God approves. Though the shards of the first tablets are broken, they are carried in the ark, along with the second tablets as a reminder of the world that was lost. But they are kept to represent an ideal, though acknowledged as unattainable. Only the second tablets of loss, creativity, and difference remain.

Trauma brings forgetting, doubt, and an anxiety that takes refuge in extremes. But, as Shakespeare's Rosalind says in *As You Like It*, 'Those that are in extremity are abominable.' It is easier, and certainly more comforting, to take refuge in the extreme of having it all, or even the certainty of having nothing. The recognition of loss in the service of memory – 'Sometimes the Torah has to be undone for it to be sustained' – allows for continuation through facing up to loss. This is the creative mourning of Otniel, engaged with the past, but looking towards the future.

The analyst, Freud writes, requires an attitude of free-floating attention. A good therapist, or friend, or spouse for that matter, will look toward the other, but also will tolerate uncertainty, not knowing. The unconscious, in Freud's secular theology, is infinite. Freudian interpretation is one that allows, by listening carefully, for the possibility of being surprised. Torah, infinite and eternal, also requires a form of free-floating attention. So the Talmud, with its apparent lack of structure, associative and expansive, sometimes seems like an inter-generational form of free-association. Learning Torah means attentiveness to the past, but without fixation, embracing uncertainty on a way to truth. There is no grasping the infinite and eternal, for there is no such thing in a world of loss. But there is still the possibility of the '*hiddush*,' or innovative perspective, the highest value in Jewish learning and life: an insight with its origins on Mount Sinai, but also utterly contemporary and new.

Part III Time and memory

The most famous meal in the Bible – Jacob's pot of lentils. As the sages fill in the details of the story, Jacob's brother Esau comes from the field hungry and asks him about the red stew: Esau wonders, 'Who died?' He knows that lentils are the food of mourners. 'Our grandfather, Abraham.' Esau pauses, 'Our grandfather is dead?' Jacob nods, as Esau composes himself and proclaims, 'If Abraham is dead, there is no Judge and no Justice.' After this, Esau sells his birthright – he is the oldest – to his brother Jacob.

Esau never thought that Abraham would live forever. Abraham had told his children and grandchildren of the covenant that God had sealed with him, and that his descendants would inherit the Land of Israel: 'I am the Lord that brought you out of *Ur Kasdim* to give you this Land to inherit it.' Esau knew this and also the part of the prophesy that anticipated his grandfather's death at 'a ripe age.' There was still another part of God's message that Esau remembered, that Abraham's offspring were to be enslaved as 'strangers in a strange land' where they would be 'oppressed and enslaved for four hundred years.' Esau as first born thought that he would bear the brunt of exile. 'Not for me,' he thought. So he 'ate, drank, got up and left, and scorned his birthright.'

From Esau's perspective, so long as Abraham was alive; so long as the family dwelled together in the Land of Israel; so long as God's presence was immediately felt, then he could believe in the 'one true Judge and his Justice.' But when Abraham dies and there is the likelihood of exile, Esau turns aside, asserting that there is 'no Judge and no Justice.' He casts the birthright aside: better to enjoy, to eat and drink. 'Pass the lentils,' he tells his brother. Seize the day for tomorrow we die. Enjoy the present: *'Carpe Diem.'*

But Jacob is different. His faith is born when God's presence is no longer immediate. Abraham is the patriarch who departs from his homeland for the Land of Israel; Isaac never leaves the Land. Jacob is the patriarch who goes into exile. Jacob agrees to buy the birthright with the knowledge that the exchange of physical pleasures – the pot of lentils – for the birthright will result first in exile, and, only after, in the inheritance of the Land.

So Esau may believe with certainty that his grandfather's seed will eventually inherit the Land. Just as assuredly as the 'tick' of a clock is followed by a 'tock,' Esau knows that the descendants of Abraham will receive their portion. But the sound a clock makes (or used to make) consists not of two parts, but three: the tick, the tock, and the interim between. Tick, as the literary critic Frank Kermode writes, may be a 'humble beginning,' and tock an equally humble ending, but together, with what comes between, they give a shape to time. The duration between the 'tick' and the 'tock' – between the promise of redemption and its fulfillment – lasts too long for Esau. The in-between forebodes too much hardship. But Jacob, when he purchases the birthright, shows himself ready to suffer exile. He maintains what Kermode calls a 'sense of an ending,' even in darkness.

Jacob embodies the faithful waiting of Israel – even after Abraham is dead – without any immediate prospect of redemption, only suffering. There is a 'tock' in the continuation of Jewish history beyond the life of Jacob and the inheritance of the Land. In this story, 'tick' is Genesis, 'tock,' the End of Days, the coming of the Messiah, *Mashiah*, or messenger of God. Sometimes the wait, the duration between the 'tick' and the 'tock,' seems interminable. So long, we may forget the end: 'Is this the promised end?' Kent in Shakespeare's *King Lear* asks anxiously. The answer always seems to be, for Lear, for us, not yet.

When Maimonides lists his thirteen principles of faith, the twelfth is the belief in the Messiah who proclaims the End of Days and a new divine dispensation on earth: 'I believe with perfect faith in the coming of the *Mashiah*.' But in an uncharacteristic expansiveness, Maimonides continues, 'and even though he delays, with all of this, I will wait, every day, for him to come.'

The duration between the 'tick' and the 'tock' does seem to be without end. Yet even though he delays – 'with all of this' – this is the Maimonidean expression of faith, 'I will wait.' 'With all of *this*.' If a principle of faith can be poignant and poetic, this qualifies. '*This*' – this is what Esau will not bear, the suffering, the anguish, the waiting for redemption. Yet the children of Israel, with 'all of *this*' they declare, they will nonetheless wait 'every day' for him to come. And how much of '*this*' there has been.

My twelve-year-old daughter asks: 'Is *Mashiah* coming?'

'Yes, he is.' 'We want *Mashiah* now!'

We are a generation of instant gratification, even, or especially, when it comes to *Mashiah*. Children can afford the attitude. But as adults, when it sometimes seems like there is 'no Judge and Judgment,' like the clock has permanently stopped, and that the 'tock' will never come, we teach our children, and ourselves, not to be like Esau. For with the sensibility of instant gratification comes inevitable disappointment, and the indulgence in the pleasures of the moment dressed up in Esau's resigned '*carpe diem*!' Yes, *Mashiah* is coming. But we also know – we have been schooled – in the fine art of waiting. 'With all *this*' – with Jacob – we still believe.

32 The antidote for religion: Fear of God

The wife of a friend is in the *schmatta* – clothing – business. She makes the *schmattas*; he collects the money and deposits it in the bank. One day recently, he took the profits of 800 shekels which, unknown to him, fell out of his pocket as he motored from one end of town to the other. I met him the following day – his remorse already turned to relief: '*Barukh Hashem*'; Thank God! – his wife had secured a new order 'the *very next day* – for *exactly* 800 shekels!'

Barukh Hashem – Thank God! – an expression of the gratitude for kindnesses bestowed. But proclamations like this one – 'The very next day she received an order for exactly 800 shekels' – can transform from acknowledgment of the past into a theology about the future. When we anticipate that God will always act in like manner; when we claim to know how God rewards and punishes; when we decide we understand His providence, then we sneak idolatry into the Temple. Not rocks and pillars that elicit our idolatrous desires, but, in our generation, money and reputation, and perhaps even more – and less detectably – our conceptions of time and the stories about the future which we like to tell.

'Adulthood,' writes Adam Phillips, 'is when it begins to occur to you that you may not be leading a charmed life.' Being an adult, breaking the spell of charms means freeing oneself of the stories of the future in order to live in the present.

God admonishes Israel to distance themselves from 'charmers' and 'observers of times,' and then enjoins: 'Be perfect with the Lord your God.' The Jewish people are told to distance themselves from the idols and ideologies of the world, and to be pure in their trust of God. But the charms of the still idolatrous nations are tempting. John Milton knew this, writing in *Paradise Lost* of a 'pleasing sorcery' that 'could charm/ Pain for a while or anguish, and excite/ Fallacious hope.' Satan's charms ward off – momentarily – pain and anguish, but only through instilling a false and misleading hope.

Freud found fearful memories of past pain to be at the root of the religious impulse. People (as Phillips explains Freud) are not bad, they are simply frightened. Fear is the response to absence, trauma, lack of love and security. It is the first fear of childhood when parental love and security, feelings of wholeness are sundered and lost. Trauma, in this Freudian story, is at the beginning, in one form or another, of every personal history. Religion provides, in the simple Freudian reading, a benevolent future of consolation, a charm to forget 'pain for a while.' In Phillips's take on Freud, one might say to the patient, 'tell me what you fear and I will tell you what has happened to you.' In this depressing vision, the experience of remembered wounds and loss makes one imagine a future limited by those failures. Even though the vision is grim, the consolation – the future will be just like the past – is relinquished responsibility: I give in to my idolatrous vision of an impossible future in which my passivity is blameless. In jumping to conclusions about the future, I close it off. Since the future will inevitably look like the past – 'things never work out for me' – I am justified in doing nothing.

There is another form of idolatry in which the analyst might say otherwise: 'Tell me what you *pretend not to fear*, and I will tell you what has happened to you.' This is the idolatry that sometimes stands in for, even pretends to look like, religious observance. In fantasies of an always benevolent future – the recovered 800 shekels as a theological statement – there are similar fears, also closing off possibilities the future may hold. This is the 'charmed' life of salvation if not always achieved, at least anticipated. My fears, in this version, put me under a self-induced spell. Things, I tell myself – or lie to myself – will always work out.

Adulthood, however, means breaking the spell, though it is easier to live a charmed life, even to pretend to do so. The charm, however, sometimes wears off in the shock of a reality denied, suddenly asserted. Such recognition, coming too late, leads not to adulthood, but crisis. So one passes directly from childhood to midlife crisis – it can happen – without the benefit of passing through adulthood. The 800 shekels is not always forthcoming; our lacks are never fully compensated.

But there are those who seem to need to affirm that God always acts with benevolence in ways which are immediately and palpably available, fulfilling our childish expectations.

Hiding in the stories that affirm a simplistic, though not simple, faith is the fear of a future that might just be like the past. We all know that past, not only of our personal histories, but the recent history of the Jewish people. Yet after the trauma of the past century, there is the desire for the self-induced spell, a charm to push off our 'pain and anguish.' So we insulate ourselves from the present in our retellings – our charmed stories – about the future. The philosopher T.W. Adorno writes, 'no poetry after Auschwitz,' lamenting language's inability to express what Conrad's Kurtz in *Heart of Darkness* calls, 'the horror.' Yet many in our generation choose not the poetry of Homer, Shakespeare, or Goethe, but Satan's *ersatz* and unsatisfying charms. How much longer can these charms satisfy? Even as we try to charm ourselves with such stories, we probably know deep down that it is just a spell.

At its deepest roots and most ancient beginning, Judaism is a form of skepticism: Abraham was the first *hozer be-she'ela* – the commonly used term in Israel to describe once observant Jews who return to a life of questioning. But being a *hozer be-she'ela* has always been at the heart of the Jewish experience. If there were more *hozerei be-she'ela* – and here is the paradox – there might be fewer *hozerei be-she'ela*. For, in many ways, the atheist has more in common with the servant of God than the idolater. He has refined the impulse of iconoclasm and cleared out the idols and 'charms,' but just fails to see his own atheism as the last remaining idol in the sanctuary.

'Be perfect with the Lord your God.' Break the idols. The Torah enjoins, as Rashi explains, not to look into the future, but 'to anticipate only God.' While the idolatrous nations are 'time-observers,' seeking propitious moments, wearing amulets and red-strings around their wrists, and consulting religious-looking astrologists and charmers, the Torah commands: 'Give them up; live in the present.' In Onkelos' Aramaic translation, the injunction of 'to be pure' is to be pure 'in *fear* of God.'

Freud is right. Religions are born out of fear; they are ideologies, claiming to provide clear and predictable maps of an already foretold future. The 'fear of God' required by the Torah is an *antidote* to religion, or to that religious impulse, and its charms, created by fear. Judaism, however, is neither an ideology nor a religion. For being perfect in the fear of God means facing a future without certainty. There are no charms, for the Jewish adult, to ward away such fears.

Twice daily, from the month preceding *Rosh Ha-shana*, the Jewish New Year to the end of *Sukkot*, observant Jews recite psalm twenty-seven. For years, I read this verse with perplexity: 'When my mother and father forsake me, then God will take me up.' Do parents *really* forsake their children? What could be further from our minds?' But parents, even the best of us, are always forsaking our children. That forsaking begins, as Rashi explains, at the time of conception – the time of the parents' 'pleasure' – after which 'they turn their faces,' and God is left to sustain the growing fetus on His own. The lonely self begins life in embryo while parents turn to different pleasures and obligations. As the child gets older, parents will sometimes, if not inevitably, turn their faces. The baby is crying, but the kettle is boiling. And the child, nurtured even by Winnicott's 'good-enough parents' who nurture their infant to childhood, and their child into adulthood, feels forsaken, left alone, and fearful. There is no 'charm,' despite the protest of Milton's Satan, to 'respite or deceive, or slack the pain.'

Be pure. Live in the present; give up the charmed stories about the future that the idolaters of the world entertain. In the reading of the Maharal, the verse is conditional, but fulfilled automatically. Be perfect in your fear of God: and when that fear of God replaces the fears that generate idolatrous stories that close off the future, *then* God will be your portion. Such a portion, however, is only for those adults willing to give up on the charmed life.

33 Speech in exile and the voice of the *shofar*

Rosh Ha-shana, the Jewish New Year is the anniversary of the creation of man. On the sixth day of the Creation, man was inspirited by the divine, and given a soul: 'And the Lord God formed man of the dust of the ground, and breathed into his nostrils the breath of life; and man became a living soul.' From the divine breath and the dust of the earth – the coming together of upper and lower worlds – man is born, the 'living soul.' Onkelos renders the latter phrase as 'speaking soul.' For man lives by virtue of his speech or *dibbur*. Yet the service on the two days of *Rosh Ha-shana* gives precedence to the *kol shofar*, the sound of the *shofar*. The Days of Awe – between the New Year and the Day of Repentance, *Yom Kippur* – begins with *kol* or sound. *Rosh Ha-shana*, the day which the Torah calls *yom teruah*, the day of the sounding of the *shofar*, is a day of sound, not yet of speech.

All of the holidays – *mo'adim* – in the Jewish calendar include special *musaf* or additional prayers. The additional prayers of *Rosh Ha-shana* make it the longest service of the year with three separate sections, on 'Kingship,' 'Remembrance', and '*Shofar*.' The blessing that ends the last section on '*Shofar*' reads: 'For You hear the voice of the *shofar* and You give ear to the *shofar* blast, and none is comparable to You.' Maimonides writes that the *shofar* arouses man to repent – 'to awaken us from the slumber of habit and draw us close to our Creator.' That the blessing emphasizes God who hears the *kol shofar* reads strangely – for it is the people of Israel, not God, who are instructed to blow the ram's horn and heed its call. The conclusion of the blessing – 'no one is comparable to You' – is no less striking. For while we find God's singularity stressed everywhere in Judaism, only in the blessing on *Rosh Ha-shana* is God's uniqueness spelled out.

Before speech comes *kol* or voice; for *kol* comes in a place where speech is not yet possible. When the people of Israel descend to Egypt, speech too, the kabbalists say, goes into exile. This is not to imply there was no conversation in Egypt. To the contrary, there was an

abundance of conversation: about the stock market, political cam-
paigns, and pennant races – all of them important, but in Egypt the
only topics of discussion. Because of the enslavement to a culture of
work and idolatry, the people of Israel forsook their tradition, leaving
its traces in their speech.

Dibbur, speech, and Betzalel's special kind of creative knowledge,
da'at, are linked: language, like *da'at*, unifies spirit and body bringing
together heaven and earth; through speech, the physical universe is
also elevated, redeemed. But when speech is in exile, it ceases to achieve
its higher purpose. Though immersed in the decadence of Egypt, the
people of Israel were still able to call out to God: 'And God heard
the cries of the people Israel.' For even when speech is corrupted, the
internal voice remains, the authentic *kol* of the soul, the *neshama*. A
person may not know how to pray, he may not know how to study
Torah, but he can still access his voice or *kol*. *Kol* is the inner voice of
longing, evidence of the residual connection to the divine.

But the *kol* in the *Rosh Ha-shana* prayers also expresses God's
longing for man where revelation and the sound of the *shofar* are
linked. For God's revelation – as the *Rosh Ha-shana* prayers show – is
linked throughout history with the *shofar*, eliciting the self-revelation
of man. The *shofar* sounded at the revelation of Mount Sinai, also associated with the day of man's creation, will also sound at the End of
Days when the final great *shofar* blast signals the full and ultimate
revelation to all humanity. Though associated with these moments of
cosmic significance, for the sages, the *shofar*, though just a physical
object, is likened to the 'inner depths of man.' The ram's horn connects
to these depths because it is the means to attend to God's revelatory
voice and draw close to Him. The *shofar* arouses us from our own
slumber of habit, from the exile of speech, and from our exile from
ourselves. *Rosh Ha-shana* not only puts us in mind of God's revelation
throughout history, but is also the day of the revelation of the inner
self, brought forth by the *shofar*, for which God yearns.

At the end of the prayer services on both days of the New Year, there
is a list of entreaties to God one of which is: 'Today seek us out for
good.' The plea to God is not only to seek good *for* us, but to seek for

the good *in* us. Seek out the good in us which other people do not know; seek out the good in us about which we ourselves do not fully know, or have forgotten. *Rosh Ha-shana* not only stresses God's 'remembrance' of His people, but what follows, man's remembrance of himself through hearing the sound of the *shofar*, and the sound of his authentic internal voice. God, as the blessing of 'Remembrance' reads, finds Ephraim to be his 'most precious son,' his 'most delightful child.' But Ephraim was also the most wayward of sons, worshipping idols. Yet God finds him to be the most precious. God longs for Ephraim, as the prayer reads, with 'His inner self,' literally His innards. God's own internal desire, as it were, is for us to reveal the internal voice, the *kol* within. We implore God during the year, but especially during the days of repentance, to hear us: 'Hear our voices.' 'Hear our authentic voices.' Attend to the voice which gets lost in our daily routines, lost to others, lost even to ourselves. The end of exile from speech begins with a return to *kol*. On *Rosh Ha-shana*, we take the first step to reclaiming our speech, by first finding the *kol*, the ability to cry out with the voice of our true selves.

This is the uniqueness of God, emphasized in the prayer: 'There is none like You.' He hears our attempts to connect to Him through the sounding of the *shofar*. God is the one who hears us and accepts our prayers. The *shofar* blasts call out: remember our authentic selves, even if we may have forgotten them. Hear our voices; help us – during these days – to remember who we are. Let us, with the *shofar* blast, recall that first 'blast' of God's breath, that inspirited us, and brought us into being, the memory of which inspires a new future. On the Days of Awe, we move from *kol* to *dibbur*, from the voice of the *shofar* to the articulate speech of *Yom Kippur*.

There are two kinds of people in the world, a friend remarked: neurotics who dwell on the past, and those who have the good sense to ignore the past and move forward. Everyone, after all, has skeletons in their closet, and to dwell on past misdeeds seems a sour and pointless activity. Even more, the burden of the past – of transgressions or dysfunction and obstinate devotion to self-destructive behavior – makes repentance seem an impossible ideal. Most Christian models of repentance, for example, realistic about the weight of transgression and seeing man, as John Milton writes, 'forfeit and enthralled/ By sin to foul and exorbitant desires' requires an intermediary 'to expiate,' in Milton's words, man's 'Treason.' The Christian theologian may say: 'The depravity of man cannot be overcome; place your faith in a redeemer able to satisfy divine anger by whose miraculous grace alone repentance is granted.' In this model, one passively acknowledges – and feels mournful for – a sinful past, relying upon God to grant atonement through a mediator that takes on the otherwise unforgivable sins of man.

Yom Kippur is the day which makes the intervention of the Christian redeemer unnecessary, and moves away from a conception of repentance as exclusively passive. 'How happy are the people of Israel. Before whom do you render yourself pure? Who purifies you?' So Rabbi Akiva asks, and answers, 'Your Father in Heaven,' citing a verse from Ezekiel: 'And I sprinkled upon you purifying waters, and you became pure.' The sage gives an additional source for his principle from Jeremiah where God is called '*Mikveh Yisrael*,' the waters that purify Israel. 'As a *mikveh* or ritual bath purifies the impure,' Rabbi Akiva explains, 'so the Holy One purifies Israel.' God is the one who cleanses Israel of her sins.

True, those who ask God to sprinkle His purifying waters upon them are passive. But the metaphor of God as the *mikveh* of Israel implies activity. God is associated with the purifying waters of the *mikveh*, but human action is necessary, finding the *mikveh* and immersing oneself. The two Biblical verses give retrospective meaning to Rabbi Akiva's two questions: 'Who purifies you?' and 'Before whom do you render yourself pure?' God is an actor, but so is man, the latter making himself pure though placing himself in the presence of God. A convert to Judaism marks his change of status – a new identity – through immersion in a *mikveh*. God is the *mikveh* of Israel, and on *Yom Kippur* the people of Israel also undergo a change in identity, through an activity which they initiate.

'Great is *teshuva*,' repentance, says Reish Lakish, 'for deliberate transgressions are accounted meritorious deeds,' as the prophet Ezekiel says, 'when the wicked man shall turn from his wickedness and do that which is lawful and right – through them he shall live.'

Past misdeeds become the source of life – 'through them,' 'even his transgressions,' according to Rashi, 'he shall live.' Transgressions are turned into merit, not through a divine hocus-pocus, turning bad deeds into good, but by an act of integrating the soul, made possible, in the Jewish conception of repentance, through a conception of time, both cosmic and personal.

Shakespeare's Macbeth presents a version of time that many of us may adopt either consciously or otherwise (tell me what you think about time, and I will tell you what you believe). For Macbeth, there is only the 'tomorrow, and tomorrow, and tomorrow' of successive and meaningless moments leading the 'way to dusty death.' Macbeth's time is now popularized on t-shirts as – in paraphrase – 'stuff happens.' But *teshuva* is based upon a notion of time in which past, present, and future come together. The *shofar* blasts on *Rosh Ha-shana* resonate with the first blast of breath inspirited into man by God at the Creation; with the sounds of the *shofar* on Mount Sinai at the giving of the Torah; and with the final *shofar* blast that comes at the end of time. The present is no longer part of a chain of separable and unrelated moments, but rather infused with the knowledge of a future when the *shofar* at the End of Days announces the redemption of humanity. The future – our ideal image of it – enters the present and even the past.

In the resonances of the *shofar* on *Rosh Ha-shana* we hear, as Rabbi Joseph Soloveitchik says, 'the evanescent moment transformed into eternity' or what Kermode calls 'the fullness of time.' On the Days of Awe, the sound of the ram's horn resonates with cosmic history – history with a beginning, middle, and leading toward an end.

This consciousness of time, initiated on *Rosh Ha-shana*, makes the *teshuva* of *Yom Kippur* possible. Not only does the nation have an ideal image of its future, but each individual also has a personal future ideal (*teshuva does* entail idealism). Just as the End of Days invests the present with meaning for the people of Israel, so the ideal future of the individual connects to the present as well as the past. Through the retrospective glance of *teshuva*, the past – now not just neurotic obsessions weighing down the self – can be transformed. But *teshuva* as idealism does not mean envisioning repentance with naïve and unthinking optimism; *teshuva* is not a divine fiat, nor is it a human one.

Maimonides describes the three parts of repentance that correspond to past, present and future. The articulate speech of *Yom Kippur* entails a verbal confession acknowledging past wrongs, an expression of present regret, and a pledge to undertake a different future. Only after acknowledging the past and showing regret can the ideal future transform transgressions into merits. Although the three parts of *teshuva* may reflect awareness of different parts of time, they happen simultaneously, paralleling the events of history which, from God's perspective, also 'happen' at once. For *teshuva* is a process of what Jonathan Lear calls in a psychoanalytic context 'integration,' of bringing the parts of the self together. There can be no insistent or hysterical declarations – 'Now I am different' – but rather introspection and integration, taking responsibility for the past, and the self.

Teshuva does not work without acknowledging the past; it certainly will not be effective when wrongs to others are not redressed. But taking responsibility for my past undoes the conventional relation of cause and effect. In the unconventional causality of *teshuva*, past actions do not bring about future events, but rather the ideal of an unrealized future re-creates the past. As Rabbi Soloveitchik writes, instead of 'event A leading to event B, B leads to A' so that a life-story is not determined, but subject to change. 'Man cancels the law of identity' with *teshuva*; in repentance, the self become nonidentical to the self it once was. As Maimonides asserts, the penitent should say, 'I am no longer the person who did those deeds.'

But *teshuva* is an ambivalent business, because though I regret my past deeds, and I have a new identity – Rabbi Akiva uses the metaphor of the *mikveh* for a reason – I must also acknowledge that I am who I am now because of who I once was. My imagined future was generated by *my* desires and, this is Reish Lakish's insight, even by my former transgressions. Protests of unworthiness or calls for absolution from an intercessor show passivity in relation to the demands of *both* God *and* the self. Atonement may be a divine dispensation, but requires a creative act that starts with acknowledging that my past, no matter how unpleasant and seemingly recalcitrant, is my own. It is true that I did bad things, but my motives, and even the actions themselves, were not all bad, or at least, not irredeemably so. *Teshuva* works because human intentions are never simple or singular, and are open to reframing. The retrospective glance reveals that my undignified past and willful transgressions are not only consistent with, but they have actually propelled me toward, a future which I had not imagined. Actions I thought had most distanced me from God now bring me close to Him. Refined by the image of my ideal self, my past misdeeds, reclaimed as my own, shape my present so they now have the power to help me realize an ideal future. I am no longer stuck with either obsessing about my past or abandoning it – both are choices of the nonintegrated self. Moving toward the future, the past recast in its light, my present is transformed. Through the power of *teshuva* transgressions become good deeds: they are the source of a new and altered life, and only through them, in the words of the prophet, do we live.

In the seventies, at Temple Sinai in Long Island, there was always full attendance for the High Holiday services, sometimes standing room only. But between *Yom Kippur* and *Simhat Torah*, *Sukkot* was the forgotten holiday. True, there was the hut, just next to the synagogue library, with the greenery and some dried-out old branches. Not even my Hebrew School teacher had much to say about the cabin with the strange roof, the willow and myrtle leaves bound with the palm frond, nor what looked like an unripe, and slightly disfigured lemon. It all seemed more of a display from the Museum of Judaism than anything lived or real – an anthropological curiosity.

In my current Jerusalem neighborhood, before I have the chance to fully digest my bagel with tuna salad after the *Yom Kippur* fast, there is the sound of hammers knocking on two-by-fours, lasting well into the night. Not only in Israel: while others close their summer houses in the Hamptons for the winter, Jews ready to sojourn out of doors, even with the beginnings of a winter chill in the air. *Sukkot*, more than any of the other holidays, is '*z'man simhateinu*,' the time of our joy. That joy expresses itself at the time of the harvest, not through focusing on the contented satisfaction of spiritual and material wealth, but leaving the comfort and safety of our homes for seven days to dwell in the *sukka*. All that divides between us and the night sky is the *sekhakh* – the branches, palm branches and twigs – that covers the walls of the *sukka*. Though one of the Torah's names for the holiday is the 'festival of gathering,' the covering of the *sukka* is made from the *by-products* of the harvest. Not the ripe ears of corn and grape vines – whole fruits – but the remnants left on the threshing floor, or on the side of the field or vineyard. The joy experienced on *Sukkot* is indeed paradoxical, arising from the knowledge that the security of the Jewish people is realized through an avowed vulnerability. A strange joy: 'vanity of vanity,' we read in Ecclesiastes on the Sabbath of the intermediate days of *Sukkot*. Some say that the reading of the book of Ecclesiastes with its vision of mortality – 'a time to live and a time to die' – modulates the *simha,* the joy, of *Sukkot.* But reading the Ecclesiastes on the holiday may stress that our joy comes from understanding that what others trust – and that in which we ourselves often place our faith – are 'vanities.'

Going into the *sukka*, the sages say, is like going into *galut*, exile. Only in exile do I realize what really sustains me; only in exile do I acknowledge that what I thought had supported me, what looked to be the most solid, is most fleeting. After finishing a meal in the *sukka*, in the blessings that follow, we call out: 'May the Compassionate One raise up the fallen *sukka* of David!' The eternal kingdom of David is compared not to great towers or monuments of empire, but to a fallen *sukka*, a bunch of wooden planks which make up a couple of walls, and some old branches. The greatest king of Israel is called the 'fallen one.' David's kingdom is eternal even in apparent defeat, and in the vulnerability of David's *sukka* lies its triumph.

When a house is re-built after it falls, it is considered a new house, no longer the same structure. A *sukka*, however, is different: though the *sukka* may fall, once the covering, the *sekhakh*, is put back in place, it retains the status of the *sukka* it once was. Though defeated and fallen and to the eye dispersed, the kingdom of David, like a fallen *sukka*, remains ready to be rebuilt. The covering of the *sekhakh*, what the Maharal calls 'the connection to the Above,' defines the *sukka*. Acknowledging the transience of what appears to be most solid – the external structures, conventional signs of wealth and power – allows a turning inward to find the permanence of the internal connection to the divine. Even if the *sukka* is fallen, the *sekhakh* scattered, it can be gathered again. For the fallen *sukka* of David is eternal.

Sukkot comes at the end of the cycle of holidays that begins with Passover, the birth of the people of Israel, and continues with *Shavuot*, the giving of the Torah on Mount Sinai. Not only the culminating part of the story told in the three major festivals of pilgrimage, when the Jews dwell, at last, under divine protection in the desert, *Sukkot* also comes as an end to the holidays of the new year which began with the Days of Awe. In this overlapping story of endings, the festival of gathering is not just the harvesting of autumn crops, but a bringing together, a gathering of the spiritual 'harvest' enacted from *Rosh Ha-shana* and *Yom Kippur*.

Sukkot is associated with endings, both national and personal. The reading from the books of the Prophets on the holiday is from Zechariah – describing the war of the nations of Gog and Magog against Israel at the End of Days. According to Rabbi Samson Raphael Hirsch, the war with Gog and Magog, the nations of the West, represents the struggle between the *sekhakh* of the temporary *sukka* and the '*gag*' or 'roof' present in the root letters of the warring nations' names. The salvation of the kingdom of David comes through what seems to be most temporary but, in the end, endures longest. In the words of the prophet, 'And it will come to pass, that every one that is left of all the nations which came against Jerusalem shall even go up from year to year to worship the King, the Lord of hosts, and to keep the festival of *Sukkot*.' The triumph of Jerusalem is marked by the universal celebration of *Sukkot*, the final raising of the fallen *sukka* of David.

The *sekhakh* of the *sukka* may be taken from the threshing floor, but not composed of any vessel or material made by human hands or any natural products still attached to the earth. A few walls covered by the branches of the old willow tree is just a shed out in the forest; those same walls covered by store-made planks has a roof and not *sekhakh*. The divine architect allows for a variety of different models and budgets: you can build a *sukka* with boards of wood, panes of glass, cinder block, or even out a couple of car doors on a day-trip. But to be a *sukka*, the walls must be covered with *sekhakh*. For *sekhakh* nullifies the two forces which detract from trust in God and faith in His guidance: nature and human ingenuity. The *sukka* both undermines a belief in nature as an uncontrollable all powerful force, a destiny beyond control, as well as the belief that human inventiveness alone – represented by technology – shapes our destinies.

One of the lessons of the *sekhakh* is to push aside belief in the fatalistic determinism of nature. The other lesson – 'Do not cover your *sukka* with the products of human ingenuity' – what the verse in Deuteronomy calls the belief in 'the strength and power of my own hand,' may be easier to internalize at a time when the security, as well as securities, upon which we have built our trust are failing. Houses have fallen, ones in which we once placed our trust – and trusts – Lehman Brothers, Merrill Lynch, Bear Stearns. Housing prices have gone down as well. The NASDAQ falls and seems to keep falling and falling. This is the time to go into the *sukka* – into what the sages call the *tzila de-hemenuta* – the shades of faith.

Gazing at the booth from the Temple library window, with the jaded and skeptical eye of the cultural anthropologist, is not enough. The *sukka* is not just a symbol, as many Jews, trying to distance themselves from the embarrassment of ritual or the appearance of commitment, sometimes claim. But like all Jewish holidays, *Sukkot* is an existential exercise in consciousness-changing, enacted through the experience of eating, drinking, sleeping, and feeling joy – maybe even an ice cream sundae party with the kids – in the paradoxical security of exile that lasts for seven days.

After a week in the *sukka*, we may understand that though not insured by AIG, the *sukka* is still the most secure place to be.

Our policy is with another Agent.

Birthright, an organization that arranges trips for young people to Israel, was recently in our Jerusalem neighborhood. We were lucky to have two guests for lunch who, like most of the participants, had never been to Israel, or experienced a *Shabbos* meal with a religiously observant family.

As we were finishing off the brownies and ginger ices, one of the guests, Steve, asked, 'So what are you guys going to do for the rest of the day?' I understood this not as a question about our *Shabbos* itinerary, but rather a polite version of another question: 'Are you guys really going to sit at home and do nothing all day?' In the end, I gave a list of coming attractions: more food (which he found hard to believe); Torah learning with a *hevruta,* or study partner; a walk around the neighborhood with the younger kids; maybe a visit to family friends. But the unstated question got me thinking back to our first days of *Shabbos* observance.

My wife and I lived adjacent to Columbia University where I was getting my doctorate, on 119th Street and Amsterdam Avenue, not exactly a thriving center of Jewish life. There was a Jewish community centered around the Old Broadway Synagogue on 125th Street, but we did not then have the network of family and friends we now enjoy. The first year we were *Shabbos* observant, the Jewish New Year, *Rosh Ha-shana*, fell on a Thursday and Friday that, followed by *Shabbos,* turned into a three-day holiday. Out of his love of baseball, Ernie Banks, the old Chicago Cubs shortstop, used to say, 'Let's play two!' – a double-header. That year, it was as if God were saying to us, 'Let's play three!' For this extended holiday, we were, however, not ready; no amount of spiritual 'spring-training' would have prepared us. Refraining from work seemed merely a pointless non-activity, as Steve's question implied: 'Just sitting around and doing nothing.'

Searching for a metaphor to describe what he does as an analyst, Jonathan Lear turns to the Sabbath. The psychoanalytical encounter, he writes, is like 'an existential Sabbath.' Reading these words on the night after Steve's visit was not so much an Oprah 'aha!' moment, but more like a Freudian 'uncanny' moment – the experience of the unexpected connectedness between things. Lear turns to the Sabbath to describe the development of the psyche; I thought about taking the metaphor in the other direction, looking to psychoanalysis as a metaphor for *Shabbos*. In a metaphor, Aristotle writes, the 'unknown or half-known is described and clarified through recourse to what is better known.' With Tony Soprano's therapy already in reruns, psychoanalysis, I thought, may help to understand *Shabbos*.

Neurotics – everybody has a friend or relative in this category – have a tendency to repeat their behavior. Freud once overheard his father saying of him, 'The boy will never amount to anything'; the master of the psyche repeated this in psychodramas played out through the rest of his life. In Freud's repetitious behavior – what he describes elsewhere as 'acting-out' – he broke off relationships with colleagues, collaborators, patients, and friends, as if to say to them: 'It's not me, but *you* who has not amounted to anything.' This is what Freud calls repetition that comes in the place of remembering. Not able to remember or confront his psychic past – too painful or traumatic – Freud repeats it. But we need not to turn to Freud for examples. We have all had the feeling, at least once, that a friend or relative is not reacting to what we have said or done, but instead relating to us through the lens of another relationship, usually an unresolved one. To which we may respond – if we are not defensive and have an inkling of what is going on – 'Hey, I'm not your mother!' Unaware of the unresolved tensions that motivate him, the neurotic lives in a world of fantasy endlessly playing out the same drama. But the neurotic – think of the extreme case of Oedipus so intent on knowing that he does not know he does not know – cannot work things out because he is always talking to the wrong people.

But the 'Sabbath' of the psychoanalytic session, Lear writes, 'allows a person to take an hour's rest from normal life' in order 'to experience an interpretive breakdown' – thus allowing for a 'special conversation,' a form of interaction, unencumbered by the neurotic's habitual repetitions. Here it seems that any comparisons between the Sabbath and psychoanalysis might be best put aside. Imagine me having said to Steve: 'You see the reason we keep *Shabbos* is so that we can have an interpretive breakdown.' I am sure that would have done the trick. If someone had said that to me at my first *Shabbos* meal, I would have turned to him as Woody Allen does to Annie's psychopathic brother Christopher Walken in *Annie Hall*: 'Sorry, I have to go now, because I'm due back on the planet earth.'

But in its way, *Shabbos* does involve a form of 'interpretive breakdown' where refraining from day-to-day activities, and the habits of mind which accompany them, opens up a space for a 'new conversation.' *Shabbos* cultivates the awareness that the mindset that governs the week, especially the certainty that we are in absolute control over our destinies, is not so different from the perspective that informs the repetitious 'acting-out' of the neurotic. Oedipus thinks he controls his destiny. His interpretive breakdown comes suddenly and unexpectedly; it is too late, too traumatic. But *Shabbos* provides an alternative.

The Torah recounts the giving of the Ten Commandments twice – once in Exodus, and then again in Deuteronomy. There are many differences in the accounts, but one of the most obvious is in the fourth commandment. The Exodus version reads: '*Remember* the Sabbath Day'; while the corresponding verse in Deuteronomy reads '*Observe* the Sabbath day.' The discrepancy in the verses does not cause the sages to start an 'Advanced Institute for Biblical Criticism,' but they look to the difference as an opportunity for interpretation, explaining that the divine utterance on Mount Sinai included both 'remember,' *zakhor*, and 'observe,' *shamor*. Though there was one utterance, both commands were expressed in the single divine expression.

The Maharal explains that though 'remembering' *Shabbos* comes first, 'observing' is more important. '*Shamor*' means refraining from weekday activities; while '*zakhor*' is an active remembrance through, as the Maharal notes, the *Kiddush* recited over wine before the Friday night Sabbath meal. Without the *shamor of* refraining from labor, the *zakhor* of remembering has no effect. It just gets drowned out. You cannot, the Maharal explains, get in the car, drive to the beach, stop off for gas, go to the MacDonald's at the rest stop, and then take out your *Kiddush* cup to proclaim the special character of the day. The Sabbath is not merely an abstract ideal – something into which it was converted in the nineteenth century – but it involves, like all of the *mitzvot* an action, or in this case, *inaction*. For the remembrance of *Shabbos* to be more than merely theoretical – for it to have an impact – one has to refrain from weekday activities. Otherwise, there is too much noise from elsewhere with which the *Kiddush* – the proclamation of the holiness of the day – has to compete.

The more one repeats, Freud writes, the less one remembers. The more one repeats the same psychodramas, the less one remembers oneself. So with *Shabbos*: one refrains from the endless repetitions of weekday activities to remember that on the seventh day of Creation, God rested. But in remembering God, there is also the remembering of beginnings, and so remembering what Freud calls the psyche, or in other terms, the *neshama, the soul,* the True Self. Once I remember that self, not the one running endlessly between urgent appointments, repeating the same habitual actions with the accompanying habitual thoughts, but the self at rest, then there is the possibility of that 'special conversation.' This is not the rest of just sitting still – of hanging around being bored and doing nothing – but of a rest in time that also creates a space, from which I can get a new perspective on myself.

Shabbos, the kabbalists explain, is not only a day of rest, but a day of *dibbur* or speech. Because we rest, and remember ourselves outside of the continual dramas of the weekday world in which we knowingly (or not) are too immersed, we acquire the capacity for a new kind of speech. The proclamation of the holiness of the Sabbath day, made possible by refraining and resting, is part of that special conversation. It takes Oedipus a catastrophic interpretive breakdown. But *Shabbos* allows for the kind of breakdown, less traumatic, that makes a space for remembrance – of the self, the family and God – every single week.

'The *mitzva* of the lighting of the *Hanuka* lamp,' writes Maimonides, is a very beloved *mitzva*.' Scholars call Maimonides a 'rationalist,' but in the laws of *Hanuka*, he expresses a rare enthusiasm – not only an adjective, but even an adverb, a 'very beloved *mitzva.*' There are 613 *mitzvot* in the Torah, and many more decreed by the rabbis, but nowhere else does Maimonides evidence such enthusiasm. When one of my children shows too much enthusiasm for an activity, a sibling may ask, '*lama ata kol kakh mitlahev*?' – 'Why are you so excited,' more literally, 'Why are you so lit up?' And why is the habitually staid and rational Maimonides so 'lit up' by the *mitzva* of *Hanuka*?

'A person should be careful,' Maimonides writes further, 'to make known the miracle, and to multiply his thanks to God and praise Him for the miracles.' Maimonides refers both to 'miracle' in the singular and miracles in the plural – *nes* and *nissim* – paralleling a different seeming inconsistency in the sages. When the question is asked, 'What is *Hanuka*?' – as Rashi explains the question, 'On what basis was *Hanuka* established as a holiday?' – the sages answer, as any school child will volunteer, the miracle of the oil that lasted for eight days. Yet in the special prayers for the eight days of *Hanuka*, the miracle of the oil is not mentioned at all, only the miracle of the Jewish victory against the Greeks. In the matter of miracles, the question to Maimonides is 'How many?' and to the sages, 'Which one?'

The miracle of *Hanuka* – or the miracles – was a response to the specific threat the Greeks represented to the people of Israel. For the sages, the Greeks occupy an ambiguous position: a Torah scroll can be written and read in a synagogue in only two languages – Hebrew and Greek – but the sages forbid a father to teach his child Greek. Further, while the sages recognize the 'wisdom of the nations of the world' and the preeminence of the Greeks among them, they also associate the Greeks with the aboriginal darkness mentioned in the second verse of Genesis: 'And there was darkness on the face of the earth.' The Greeks 'with their decrees,' say the sages, 'darkened the eyes of Israel.'

The parallels and contrasts between *Hanuka* and *Purim* – the two holidays ordained by the sages – help to explain this Greek 'darkness.' On *Purim*, the Jewish people strayed through attending the feast of the Persian King Ahashveros which had been forbidden them by Mordekhai, the Jewish leader of that generation. The Jewish people transgressed with their bodies, and as a result, the punishment decreed by the King's minister Haman, was to their bodies, to kill them. That some of the Jews may have wanted to convert was of no interest: Jewish father or mother, or even grandparent, their fate would be the same. To avoid the impending threat, the Jews of Shushan appealed to God through fasting – again with their bodies. When salvation came, they celebrated with drinking and eating, as still happens today on *Purim*, as we express joy in commemoration of the miracles of Shushan through indulging in physical pleasures.

The story of *Hanuka* is different: at the end of the period of the Second Temple, the service in the Temple had lapsed. The Jews were threatened not with the destruction of their bodies, but their minds and souls. The Greeks sought to eradicate Jewish commitment to Torah and *mitzvot*. Antiochus, the Greek King, unlike Haman, sought actively to assimilate Jews to Greek universalism; and so there were Hellenized Jews, for which there are no parallels in the other exiles suffered by Israel.

Hellenizing the Jew was part of the consistent strategy of the Greeks. They might have destroyed the oil consecrated for Temple service, but instead they defiled it, leaving its external form unchanged though rendering it impure. So also, they left the outer shell of the Temple in Jerusalem standing, but gutted it of its Jewish content, turning it into a *gymanasia*, celebrating the primacy of Greek universalism. From the outside, the Jew may have looked the same, but, like the oil and the Temple, he was defiled internally. The strange exile of Greece – it is the only exile in which the Jews remained in the Land of Israel – is the internal exile of assimilation. The Greeks turned sacred into secular: they were *mehallel*, and so created a literal *halel* or void in the souls of the people of Israel. In response to this danger, the Jews, led by the _kohanim_ or priests, rededicated their souls – they were _moser nefesh_ – to divine service. So when salvation came after these trials, the Jews celebrated not through food and drink as in Purim, but with thanks and praise to God.

Praise or _hoda'a_ is connected to _hod_ or beauty. The kabbalists write that the eight days of _Hanuka_ are days of _hod_ so the days of _Hanuka_ are days of both praise and beauty. _Hod_ and _hoda'a_ imply flexibility, even dependence. To praise God is to recognize a reliance upon a force outside of the self. Similarly, _hod_, unlike _yofi_, the external beauty the Torah associates with the Greeks, implies vulnerability or yielding. The _hod_ of Moses' splendorous face in the Book of Numbers as he descends from Mount Sinai is not the external beauty of the Greeks, but an external sign of an inner state. _Hod_ is a beauty that breaks forth from the physical world, yielding to a force beyond it.

The beauty of _Hanuka_ is in the _hod_ of the _Hanuka_ lamp, burning for eight days. Ask Aristotle or Isaac Newton how long the lamp will burn. Both will say: one day. The lamp that burned for eight days shows a force beyond both Aristotelian and Newtonian laws of physics. The Greeks are the 'darkness' of a world limited by empirical observation. Maimonides writes that the Greeks were the first of the nations to live in a world without _any_ service. Other nations of the world may have worshipped strange gods, but the Greeks were godless. They darkened the eyes of the Jews, habituating them to a world governed by the laws of nature, a world exhausted by what can be immediately experienced and measured.

So Maimonides writes: be careful to make the miracle, _in the singular_, known: this is the miracle of the oil, the miracle which the eight days of _Hanuka_ commemorate. If you do not have candles or oil, Maimonides advises, sell your belongings – 'your coat', and in our day he might add, even your Swatch and your designer sunglasses. Even if you live in a Jewish neighborhood where there are thousands of _menorot_, _Hanuka_ lamps, and where you might easily protest: 'Of course the miracle is known – why should I sell my coat?' But making known the miracle of the oil is not a miracle directed only outwards, but also, maybe even primarily, to the self. On *Purim*, I show my love of God with my body, drinking and feasting, in the *mitzva* of drinking to a state of not knowing. *Hanuka*, by contrast, is the holiday of a refined form of knowledge, the holiday of perception.

Be careful to recognize the *hod* of the *Hanuka* lights which testify that nature is flexible, that it bends and yields to the divine. First comes the acknowledgment of the *hod* of the *Hanuka* lamps, only afterward the *hoda'a* or praise for the miracles *in the plural* of the Jewish victory. The *Hanuka* lamp is acknowledged as a miracle in and of itself. But seeing the *hod* of the light that burns for eight days allows for the perception of the miracles in the plural, the wars between Jews and Greeks that cynics might reduce to a history book example of geo-politics. It is not hard to hear the voice of Greek scoffers reducing *everything* to the laws of nature. But the sight of the *hod* of the *Hanuka* lamps leads to the *hoda'a* or praise for the Jewish military victory, as well as the continuous recognition of the miraculous character of the every day.

The *mitzva* of the *Hanuka* lamps is 'very beloved' for finding light, even *hod*, in the darkness of Greek exile. Acknowledging the *hod* of the lamp activates praises and thanks for the miracles that are less easily seen in a world the Greeks have darkened. The answer to the internal exile of Greece – which in some ways still continues today – is the light of the *Hanuka* lamp, and the alteration of perception it makes possible. So Maimonides gets 'lit up' by the lights of *Hanuka*. God transformed the oil of the lamp through which – if we see the *hod* – the world also becomes a different place. For the beauty of *Hanuka* is internal.

38 Whose letter is it anyway? Esther, Aristotle, and the art of letter-writing

The first philosophical question I considered was posed by a Saturday morning television commercial for Razzles – 'candy or gum?' My earliest brush with categorical indeterminacy, the kind of question which fascinated Aristotle: Does the man with facial hair have a beard? Or is it just a five o'clock shadow? Razzles, it turns out, depending on the perspective, is both candy and gum – no surprise there.

On *Purim*, there is another confusion of categories. The Book of Esther, or *Megillat Esther*, read in synagogue on Purim night and morning, refers to itself as both an *iggeret*, a letter, and as a *sefer*, a book. The sages point out this ambiguity: '*Megillat Esther* is both a book *and* a letter.' At the end of the *Megilla* itself, when the verses recount the *Megilla*'s own writing, the *Megilla* refers to itself as a letter. In this account, Queen Esther's name precedes Mordekhai – 'Then Esther the queen, the daughter of Avihail, and Mordekhai the Jew, wrote . . . .' But when the *Megilla* refers to itself as a 'book,' the name of Mordekhai, the leader of the Jewish community in Shushan, comes first. Not, however, only a matter of letters and books: the sages explain that the events that transpired in Persia's capitol city were recorded and catalogued in the Baghdad Library. Esther, in the telling of the sages exclaims: 'I am in the Persian Chronicles!' If Esther is already written in the Persian Chronicles, why is there a need for *Megillat Esther*? Further, whose letter – or book – is it anyway?

A book has permanence and is written for posterity; while a letter partakes of the day-to-day, the quotidian. Like all of the other books of the Torah, the scribe writing a *Megilla* will first impress lines into the parchment so that the rows of verses are evenly spaced. But when the *Megilla* is bound with other sacred texts in a scroll, including not only the five books of the Torah but the books of the Prophets and Writings as well, the *Megilla* must be on parchment of a different size. At once sacred, like all of the other books – the etching of the scribe's knife linking them together – the *Megilla* is also distinct. It may be included within the inclusive giant scroll with the other books of Torah, but if it is to be read in synagogue, the size of the parchments must show that the *Megilla* stands apart. Perhaps the ambiguous status of the *Megilla* is a part of the sages' concession to Esther: 'Take a place among the rest of the Holy Writings, but remember that your status – after all you only record current events – does not warrant a sacred scroll.'

The events which took place in the Persian capitol seem to be the stuff of the everyday, material for a letter, a newspaper, or even a blog. There are court intrigues, domestic disagreements, beauty contests, assassination attempts, sleepless nights, and lotteries. This is nothing like the rest of the Torah, nor even a successful literary work, but closer to a soap opera. In his *Poetics*, Aristotle argues for the importance of 'unity of action,' an element sadly wanting in the variety of action of the *Megilla*. To Aristotle, all parts of the story – down to the last detail – must serve the end of the plot. The poet, Aristotle says with characteristic flat-footedness, must write a story which has 'a beginning, a middle and an end.' 'The beginning is necessarily followed by something else,' Aristotle instructs; 'the middle is between the end and the beginning'; and 'the end follows after the middle.' Nothing shocking here. But Aristotle's prosaic recipe for writing – he makes being a philosopher seem easy – stresses the links between parts of the story. 'Imagine all of the events of the story before your eyes,' Aristotle advises the aspiring writer. 'If there is an episode that does not fit,' or anything 'haphazard,' he warns his author, 'dispense with it.'

The *Megilla*, by Aristotle's standards, is a seeming failure because nothing fits, as it gives a history without reason, random events strung together, episode after episode: Macbeth's 'tomorrow, and tomorrow, and tomorrow.' Passover, the first holiday in the Jewish yearly cycle, shows the providential hand of God at every turn. Even the most humble household servants saw the hand of God at the parting of the Red Sea. But in the story of *Purim* which comes at the end of the yearly sequence of holidays, there is no evidence of God's presence when the forces of evil – led by the malevolent minister Haman and abetted by the incompetence of King Ahashveros – conspire against the Jews.

The *Megilla* is the only one of the sacred books in which the divine name does not appear. In this sense, *Purim* is *the* contemporary holiday, accommodating the experience of God's absence. 'Where is Esther's name in the Torah?' the sages ask, looking for a hint of her name in the Five Books of Moses. In the verse from Deuteronomy, 'I will hide my face,' '*anokhi astir pani*.' Esther's name (*astir* has the same root letters) is hidden in God's act of hiding His face. The work that bears Esther's name is about what is *not* revealed.

Yet in the paradox of *Purim*, God's absence reveals presence as the events, portending disaster, take an unexpected direction. What had appeared to add up to an Aristotelian failure of unrelated episodes, and seemed to conspire to the destruction of the Jews of Shushan, leads to their salvation. Haman's most intricate plans turn against him and, in the end, the seemingly unrelated incidents reveal themselves to be essential to the plot. With the right perspective, the *Megilla* turns into an Aristotelian success story in which every event is necessary to the whole. This is the 'the turn-around' of the *Megilla*, in which there is, in the end, nothing 'haphazard,' as God reveals himself in unanticipated ways.

Passover is the holiday of the transparency of God's providence, *Purim* the holiday of not knowing. We are sometimes guilty of what the French psychoanalyst Jacques Lacan calls 'fixating on a cause,' closing off questions about the world or ourselves by seeing things from only one perspective. So we limit God's power and providence by assuming that our limited understanding of a story – the story in Shushan or our own – also constrains God. In the revelry of drinking and feasting of *Purim* – the *mitzva* of drinking to a point of not knowing (yes, a divine command to get drunk) – comes a special kind of knowledge, the knowing through not knowing. I thought I knew, but I did not. I thought I understood the ways of the world, how events must come to pass, but I was wrong. I express this to my fellow Jews with whom I exchange gifts of food on the day of *Purim*. Some say it is best to give these gifts through an intermediary so I do not see his face. In this act of giving, I show that I love my friend even though I do not see his face, and so I love God, even in his apparent absence. But more than that, the highest knowledge of *Purim* is the love that expresses itself through realizing that I cannot know. *Purim*, as Rabbi Shlomo Carlebach says, is the day in the year I acknowledge that claiming to fully understand – God or another person – is 'the most destructive thing in the world.' The love expressed on *Purim* for God and my fellow Jew is the love that does not have to know. But, in the end, the divine absence is only apparent. What seemed to be causes leading to destruction bring about the rescue of the Jewish people. We did not know, but the letter from Shushan – the AP headlines from Persia's capitol – form a whole we had never thought to know.

The Persian Chronicles will not do, for, as Aristotle writes, chronicles provide a list of events, but they do not tell a story. Poetry is better than history, Aristotle explains, for the historian only tells what happened, but the poet shows the links that make events happen as they do. Only Esther – she is the Aristotelian poet *and* prophet – is able to give the complete story, with the necessary connections between what had seemed like unrelated events. In those links – links I did not at first know – the unstated divine name is present. The *Megilla*, unified through the perspective of Esther, tells a story where everything fits. In the apparent randomness of events, God's providential presence is revealed.

To the question: whose *Megilla* is it anyway? The answer is: Esther's. So her name precedes Mordekhai when it comes to the verse describing the authoring of the 'letter.' But when Esther approaches the sages of her generation, asking to establish her 'letter' as part of the Holy Writings, then Mordekhai's name comes first for his role – he is the head of the Jewish high court, the Sanhedrin – in transforming the 'letter' into a 'book.' Mordekhai canonizes Esther's letter into a book for generations.

The practice in synagogue – a custom more than eight hundred years old – is to unroll the *Megilla* on the pulpit before reading it. The *Megilla* is read in this distinctive fashion, rolled out like a letter, to show that it is not like other books of the Torah. After the reading, the scroll is rolled again, showing how all the details are also rolled up and collected (the root in the word for letter, *iggeret*, also means to collect).

All who hear the *Megilla* must know that this letter/book is different from the other books of the Torah. That the *Megilla* remains distinct does not show its status as lower than the other Holy Writings. But the *Megilla* is read as a letter to emphasize that what we are reading could be – and is – on a par with reading a blog, current events. A letter may be transitory, a disposable witness to the events of daily life. The events of Shushan *are* the everyday. But after the Jews of Shushan fasted and repented, from the apparent randomness of events, the *hester panim* – God's hidden face – revealed itself. God is not limited by the stories that we tell, or even our imagination about what stories may possibly be told. When Esther balks at the prospect of going to the palace to entreat the King, Mordekhai warns, 'Salvation will come from elsewhere.' God has other options. But in the end, the salvation comes through Esther, and the letter becomes a book. Esther asked of the sages, 'Make my letter into a book.' 'Turn my account of the everyday into a book on a par with the other Holy Writings.' For the hybrid letter/book shows the way in which the everyday, and the dark repetitions of seemingly unredeemed history, also have within them – in the Aristotelian links which only Esther is able to reveal – patterns of the divine.

39 Cosmic consciousness: The Beatles, passover, and the power of storytelling

What could bring the two remaining Beatles, Paul McCartney and Ringo Starr, back together? Surprise: the David Lynch Foundation which advocates teaching Transcendental Meditation. 'Every child,' the foundation website reads, 'should have one class period a day to dive within himself.' As part of the show at Radio City, after Ringo and Paul sang a version of 'With a Little Help from My Friends,' the two performed a tune that Paul had composed on a 1968 trip to an ashram in India, 'Cosmically Conscious.' So the two former Beatles sang, 'Come and be cosmically conscious, cosmically conscious with me.'

Passover is also a time for raising consciousnesses, but when thoughts turn to Passover, they are not wholly transcendental. In all of the festival commemorations, the Exodus from Egypt is recalled. Making *Kiddush* over wine, we do not remember God as the Creator of the heavens and the earth – that would be the strictly transcendental version. We mention rather God who took the People of Israel out of Egypt, eliciting not just a cosmic consciousness, but a collective experience of lived history – from Egyptian slavery to redemption. No transcendental meditation at the *seder*, but story-telling, the reading and performance of the *hagada*. The Torah says, 'And you shall tell in the ears of your children, and of your children's children, what things I have wrought in Egypt, and My signs which I have done among them; that you may know that I am the Lord.' As the hasidic sage the Sefat Emet writes, the 'story telling' of the Torah's command, 'you shall tell your children,' brings about 'knowledge' or '*da'at*' – 'that you may *know.*' It is *da'at* which enables Betzalel, the master craftsman, to build the sanctuary in the desert, joining heaven to earth.

Try this for a thought experiment: you have been asked to create a religion, and part of that religion will be a *mitzva* – a divine command – to tell a story. It is the kind of thing a literary critic might make up. Stephen Greenblatt, one such literary critic, writes that if there is a

Eucharistic moment – when body and spirit come together for Catholics in the mass – for Jews, it is on the night of the *seder*. But the experience of the *seder* is not achieved through the metaphysical fiat of a priest, but through fathers and mothers telling their children a story. From this *mitzva* no one is exempt. So the *hagada* begins: 'Even if we are all wise, all understanding, all experienced, we are still obligated to recount the Exodus.' Even a wise person, alone on the night of the *seder*, recalls the redemption from Egypt. He stays up half the night, by himself, repeating a story that he has known and studied his whole life.

'In every generation,' we read in the *hagada*, 'each person should see himself as if he were leaving Egypt.' Maimonides in his *hagada* reads differently: 'Each person should *show himself* as if he were leaving Egypt,' stressing the performance of the Exodus, for oneself and others. The *hagada*, not only a story, is also a play, a set of stage directions for a performance enacting the redemption. The Torah instructs, 'Remember you were once a slave in Egypt.' You must imagine, says Maimonides, that you yourself were a slave in Egypt, that you left and were redeemed. Not just slogans of cosmic consciousness but an enactment: eating bitter herbs to remember the affliction of Egypt, drinking four cups of wine, and then eating *matza* while reclining in the manner of free men and women, to remember *and* relive the redemption.

So interested are the sages in the experience of the *seder*, they provide recipes for the performance. For Rabbi Yohanan, the *haroset*, the mixture of wine, nuts, and fruit, commemorates the mortar the people of Israel used for bricks to build pyramids and palaces. For Rabbi Levi, the aromatic blend recalls the apple trees under which Jewish women led their husbands who, citing the Egyptian oppression protested, 'We can't have children, not now.' Abaye gives the recipe – food can be philosophical – for a dialectical consciousness of both slavery and redemption. 'Make sure that you pound it to make it thick,' commemorating the hardship of slavery, and 'add lots of wine and apples to make it sweet,' recalling the eventual redemption. No transcendental meditation here; pass the apple peeler.

The *seder* is full of props for performance – though it is always fun to innovate, as in our house, where red dye stands in for blood,

marshmallows for hail, and toffees sometimes pelted gently at nod-
ding sleepy heads. But for the Torah and the sages, central to the
performance is speech. 'And the Lord God formed man of the dust of
the ground, and breathed into his nostrils the breath of life; and man
became a living soul.' Man, the living soul, is the creature who speaks.
Not just spiritual, he is the hybrid being, composed of both the dust
from which he was formed and the divine breath which inspirited
him. Descartes, having ruined everything for Europeans with a philosophy separating mind and body, tried to make amends by suggesting
that despite everything, the spirit does invest the physical in the pineal
gland, at the center of the brain above the spinal column. Or perhaps
it was Descartes' version of a philosophical joke. The Maharal, however – no philosophical models for him – is serious when he writes
that mind and body come together in the tongue.

Though a picture may be worth a thousand words – even the most
humble of the children of Israel experienced a prophetic vision more
vivid and intense than that of the prophet Ezekiel – on *seder* night, the
turn is primarily to words. Hearing, in its primary sense, as Onkelos
stresses, is tied to reception and internalization. Although the children
of Israel experienced what some today might call the 'visuals' on their
way out of Egypt, it was not long before they were worshipping the
golden calf. So much the more in our generation when going to the
Western Wall evokes sentiments more fitting to the concert arena – 'It
was so amazing!' – there is a need to translate 'cosmic consciousness,'
and bring it to down to earth through speech and story-telling, a live
performance leading to internalization.

That the *hagada* begins with 'the Four Questions,' asked by the
youngest child at the table, stresses that the performance on the night
of the *seder* is an intergenerational activity. The *hagada* gives guide-
lines, but the story will be told, and the questions answered differently
in each home. Through the description of the 'Four Children' in the
seder, the *hagada* acknowledges that children are different, and that
parents must tell the story of the redemption in such a way that
their own children can best hear it. Only in this way does telling of the
Exodus lead to *da'at*, a knowing that makes the abstract ideal *felt*

through experience – whether for the wise man alone in his study or for the second grader, part of the *seder* for the first time.

'One who expands on the story of the Exodus from Egypt is praise-worthy.' Those who embellish, expand – who know how to tell a good story – are to be praised. The nineteenth-century sage, the Alter of Kelm, explains that the word for praiseworthy, *m'shubah*, comes from the word '*mashbiah*' which means improved or refined. Storytelling, the annual drama of performance which includes slavery and redemp-tion, provides an opportunity for the refining and improving of the self, through *da'at*, taking that transcendental cosmic consciousness, internalizing it, and making it real.

40   Trauma's legacy: On Israel's Memorial Day

I went to Mount Herzl on the morning of *Yom ha-Zikharon*, Israel's Memorial Day, for the ceremonies at the military cemetery in Jerusalem not far from my house. In Israel, Memorial Day, instituted by the Knesset in 1948, is followed, the next day, by *Yom Ha-tzma'ut*, Israel Independence Day, commemorating the establishment of the State. The days have been called Israel's 'new High Holidays,' which is true in the sense that they have become central to Israeli identity in the modern Jewish state. In the Israeli imagination, the days move from despair to triumph – so Memorial Day is followed by Independence Day.

I have hesitations about the story implied by these two days, and especially their proximity to one another. But I took my daughter, Avital, to Mount Herzl to acknowledge the service and sacrifice on behalf of the people and the State of Israel – with 24,293 dead since its founding. It was moving and strange in a uniquely Israeli way – I recalled Clinton's shocked expression at the Rabin funeral, which was chaotic and public, and, at the same time, intimate and dignified. Bottles of water, piled in huge boxes, were offered to all by eager high school students. More young people in oversized blue jackets were positioned behind tables that held piles of flowers. Some standing closer to the entrances looked as if they wanted to sell their wares, but instead they freely dispensed the flowers to the thousands piling into the cemetery. Avital took a bunch – we would find, I told her, an unvisited grave upon which to place the flowers. We looked, but did not find one.

On Independence Day, the families who visited the cemetery the day before, gather for a family barbeque or *mangal*. As a friend relates, the controversial theological question of whether one should say *Hallel* – psalms of praise recited on traditional Jewish holidays – on Independence Day pales in importance to the barbeque. In each of the tiers of the cemetery we visited, there were families gathered. Among them, the religious border policeman in his late sixties in full uniform who had brought small collapsible chairs for himself and his wife, as well as new generations of mourners, his children and grand-children. It looked as if they had been there for decades. In the middle of the family circle – the scene was repeated again and again on all the terraced levels of graves – instead of the *mangal*, a gravestone; the family stoking not coals, but what seemed like an ancient grief. There were those whose loss was fresh – the young mother with a toddler and infant crying over a grave – but the overall impression was of a nation that has been grieving for a long time.

Rabbi Joseph Soloveitchik distinguishes between moods and emo-tions. The former, he writes, are 'homogenous and singular,' while the latter are complicated, consisting of different elements. Emotions accommodate the ambivalent complexity of experience, acknowledg-ing that, as T. S. Eliot writes, 'implicit in the expression of every experience are other kinds of experience which are possible.' The Jew, Rabbi Soloveitchik writes, should pursue a complex life of emotion and not the singularity and satisfaction offered by the mood; the latter, a quick and reactive response, offers immediate satisfactions, but can end up as vulgar, 'degrading.'

The Torah, notes Rabbi Soloveitchik, cultivates emotions and not moods. When experiencing the plenty of God's beneficence, for exam-ple, the Jew on pilgrimage to Jerusalem is commanded in Deuteronomy to remember the poor. Amidst wealth and pleasures, he remembers others; the consciousness of plenty is balanced by the knowledge of poverty and need. Similarly, when mourning the destruction of the Temple and the loss of the divine presence on the ninth of *Av*, the Jew does not say the usual penitential prayers of supplication recited dur-ing morning and afternoon prayers, for the day is a *mo'ed*, a holiday, and also anticipates the coming of the *Mashiah*, the Messiah. In this way, commemorative days on the Jewish calendar incorporate the opposite of the dominant emotion of the day. Experience of abundance brings about acknowledgment of need; the absence of the divine presence is accompanied by hope for the return of that presence at the End of Days.

In the United States, for most people, Memorial Day simply marks the beginning of the beach season in May, and, for some religious Jewish men, the day to replace a black hat with a white straw one, with Independence Day, the Fourth of July, following later. The sense of collective loss and national triumph has been muted by the passage of years, and is muted as well by the interval between the two holidays. In Israel, the proximity of the days should nurture emotions and not moods, leading to a heightened consciousness that even in national victory (avoiding the term salvation) the memory of suffering and vulnerability remains present. In some cases, it does: as with our cab driver, who stopped for the two-minute siren of remembrance that morning, limping to attention, from an 'old shrapnel wound,' as he stood outside of the cab to mourn the dead, including a seventeen-year-old brother who had been killed outside of the gates of the Old City in 1967. But the two days – each representing the singularity of one mood, despair on Memorial Day and triumph on Independence Day – sometimes discourage the sensitivity to complexity cultivated by the traditional Jewish holidays.

Trauma can lead to the fostering of moods, or to the cultivation of the complexity of emotion. The Jewish people are enjoined to remember their origins: 'Remember you were a slave in Egypt.' Such a memory is the precondition for transforming the trauma of slavery into a more refined form of consciousness. Addressed, trauma can lead to the acknowledgment of vulnerability that may ultimately promote receptivity to others. But trauma can also have a different effect: a nurtured, even cherished suffering may become license for a narcissism that turns to arrogance, redressing pain by way of asserting an impossible invulnerability. Mourning, as Adam Philips writes, can make fundamentalists of us all. The resultant stories of what the Torah calls 'my strength and my power' are asserted with a daunting unambivalence, justifying conquest. I refer not to politics, certainly not geopolitics, but to something more important – the constitution of the Israeli, or Jewish, soul.

What if, I wondered as we left the cemetery, the proximity of these commemorative days does in fact lead to an arrogant and self-justifying triumphalism? What if, in the pursuit of the nationalism of the other nations of the world, in the desire to be Israelis with a political identify rather than a Jewish one, we lose the awareness of the stranger – in ourselves and others – that defines us as a people? What if, overtaken by a mood of nationalist exuberance, we fail to transform trauma into sensitivity, and allow all of those generations of suffering – and the pain felt at Mount Herzl – to be squandered?

41 Why I gave up biblical criticism and just learned to love

I never was very interested in biblical criticism – that academic discipline, founded in the nineteenth century, promising to tell the truth about biblical authorship. Even as an undergraduate English major, the readings of Bible scholars seemed dry, clunky, and uninteresting. There has been a lot of talk about biblical criticism recently, with a new book, James Kugel's *How to Read the Bible*, claiming once and for all to provide a vision of the Bible 'as it really was.' Kugel and other biblical critics believe that if we just read the Bible scientifically, we can sift through all of the facts and evidence and have an objective picture of things. But I have never been compelled by the readings of biblical scholars with their alphabet soup of authors – J, D, P – which to me is just a way of avoiding engagement with the complexities and nuances of the Bible. I certainly would not want a biblical scholar to help me read Milton's *Paradise Lost*. Where Milton argues through paradox, they would just see contradiction – evidence for multiple authorship of the great epic.

Now is probably not the time to go into the way in which enlightenment beliefs in reason are also faith-based practices, though people like Christopher Hitchens and Richard Dawkins show a zeal for their atheist agendas which makes the faith of some of my neighbors in Jerusalem seem lukewarm. Indeed, the tenacity of unreasonable beliefs, as one of their fellow 'new atheists' calls it, may be as common among so-called nonbelievers as believers. Nor is it the place to cite those scholars in various academic disciplines – not crazy postmodernists, but respected humanists *and* scientists – who have called into question the whole notion of objective scholarly neutrality upon which biblical criticism is founded.

When discovering the Jewish tradition back in graduate school, I remember a relative – maybe my father-in-law – saying that if God had wanted to give a handbook to humanity, he would have given it in binary code. It makes a certain kind of sense. Today, he would probably suggest that God should have given Moses the Torah on a disk-on-key. To him, this would have been a form of revelation that could be objectively understood, requiring no interpretation at all. But the Torah in its very first verse asserts itself not as dry data, an objective knowledge, but revelation founded upon relationship – between God and His people, Israel. As Rashi explains the '*bereshit*' – 'In the Beginning' – of the first verse of the Torah is a contraction of *bishvil reishit*, 'on behalf of the first.' And 'the first,' as Rashi shows from passages in the Prophets and Writings refers to Torah *and* Israel. The world was created for the sake of divine revelation through Torah *and* for Israel, the latter the means through which the divine revelation comes into the world. Torah and Israel are *together* the purpose of creation; without one, the other does not exist. There is no Torah without Israel, no giving of the Torah without those able to receive it.

God did not choose Israel to be a disinterested observer, but He founded a relationship with Israel based upon love. 'With an abundant *love* you have *loved* us' – so begins the second of the two blessings which precede the recitation of the *Shema* – 'Hear O Israel' – in the morning. And in the evening blessings preceding the *Shema*: 'With an eternal *love*, you have *loved* us' – a love expressed through God's bestowing of 'Torah, *mitzvot*, decrees and law' to His people Israel. So Torah and love are linked together. The morning blessings also include an entreaty to God: 'Instill in our hearts to understand, to elucidate, to listen, learn, teach, safeguard, perform and fulfill all the words of Your Torah's teaching with *love*.' That we ask that God grant understanding to our *hearts*, and not to our minds, accentuates that this is not merely a cognitive relationship, but one based on love. The morning blessings conclude with the praise of God who brings Israel close to Him so that they can 'praise His unity with *love*,' and the benediction of 'God who chooses Israel with *love*.' A reciprocal relationship of love: the numerical value or *gematria* of the word love, *ahava*, is equal to that of another word, *echad* or one: love unifies. The act of receiving the Torah is an act of union or love. Maimonides calls the work devoted to the laws of prayer and the *Shema*, as well as to *brit mila* and *tefillin* – which show the connection between God and His people – *Sefer Ahava* or the *Book of Love*.

The sages refer to the giving of the Torah as 'the day of our marriage' – a day of union. One of the blessings from the marriage ceremony refers to five sounds – the 'sounds of joy and of gladness,' the 'sound of joyful wedding celebrations,' and the 'sounds of youthful feasting and singing' that correspond to the five 'sounds' that accompanied the giving of the Torah on Mount Sinai. That the sages compare the giving of the Torah to marriage is not just a poetic embellishment. God chooses Israel with love, and the response must be love. There is no external perspective, no possibility of disengagement, but rather learning Torah is an act of love. The *Shema* begins: 'And you shall love the Lord your God. . . .' The injunction to love God is followed by another command: 'Let these words which I command you today be upon your hearts.' Through 'these words' – learning Torah – love of God expresses itself.

The continuation of the verse in the *Shema* further refines the definition of learning Torah, and by extension the love of God: '. . . and you shall teach them to your children.' The *mitzva* of Torah study, as Rabbi Yitzhak Hutner writes, is only consummated in the teaching of children and students. There is a vertical relationship – both up and down – a double connection. With love one strives upwards to the divine, but only completes that act of love through a corresponding downward movement, bringing Torah into the world and teaching the next generation. My love of God, realized through learning Torah, reaches its perfection with the love expressed in 'you shall teach your children' – establishing a double movement of connectedness and love.

As Jonathan Lear writes, the position of objectivity and the so-called 'neutral perspective' is just a myth; attempting to occupy it leads to 'developmental failure and pathology.' We have all been there, though likely not as Miltonists or biblical critics who forestall genuine engagement with texts through their flat and preachy, always definitive and final readings. We have more likely occupied that perspective in bad moments as spouses, or equally bad moments as parents, where we flee to a place of disengaged complacency, crabbiness, and self-righteousness instead of engaging with those whom we love. 'To love or not,' Milton writes, 'in *this* we stand or fall.'

So when given the opportunity to learn Torah, we may want to lay aside that very contemporary and Western desire for objectivity and cool disengagement, and start to love a little, and, on the way, begin to make the Torah our own.

'And I will dwell upon you' – God says to the people of Israel. He dwells among them, first in the sanctuary in the desert and then in the two Temples in Jerusalem. The ninth day of the month of *Av* commemorates the destruction of both Temples, the day to which future Jewish tragedies are linked – exile, pogrom, and holocaust. 'I will hide my face from them,' and so God – Jews know too well – withdraws his presence when He turns His face from His people. Not only is the face of God absent, Primo Levi writes out of Auschwitz, but also the human face. 'I do not know who my neighbor is. I am not even sure that it is always the same person because I have never seen his face.' Auschwitz – *hurban* and destruction – is the faceless world without the presence of God or man.

The First Temple, built in the merit of the patriarchs, Abraham, Isaac, and Jacob, was destroyed on the ninth of *Av* because of the sins of the people of Israel: illicit relationships, idolatry, and murder. Abraham's *hesed*, the excess of generosity, turns into vulgar indulgence; Isaac's subjugation of his will to God, bound on the altar by his father, turns to idolatrous ritual; the peace established by Jacob, through the tribes of Israel, transforms into murder. When the attributes of the patriarchs turn to their opposite, writes the Maharal, the First Temple falls. The Temple is rebuilt, not on the patriarchs' merits, but because of the unity of the people of Israel. In the *Purim* story, Esther calls for a day of fasting: 'Go and gather all the Jews of Shushan.' As a result of their heeding her call for unity – the story of Esther takes place during the Babylonian exile – the Temple is rebuilt. As the Maharal writes, the sustenance for the First Temple came from Above, the relationship that God initiates with the patriarchs. That of the Second Temple came from below, from the people of Israel. But when the Roman general Titus destroyed the Temple hundreds of years later, also on the ninth of *Av*, the sages say that the people of Israel were engaged in Temple service, studying Torah, and performing acts of kindness – what Simon the Just later calls the 'three pillars upon which the world stands.' There may have been scrupulous observance to the Torah, and even shows of care for others, but beneath it all, there was baseless hatred. And so the Second Temple fell.

'You shall not hate your neighbor in your heart,' God commands the people of Israel in Leviticus. There is another command which must be fulfilled with all 'your heart' – '*be-khol levavcha*.' In the first verse of the '*Shema*,' God commands that one love Him with all one's heart – the doubling of the letter *bet* in the Hebrew word for heart means, the sages say, that one must love God with both good and bad inclinations. In practice, I am commanded to love God with the energies which I am happy to publicly own along with those I am less inclined to acknowledge. The sixteenth-century sage of Safed, the Alsheikh, applies the words of the sages about love of God to the command to refrain from hating one's neighbor, as both commands are incumbent on the heart. Just as I love God with both good and bad inclinations, I also hate with both inclinations. To hate a neighbor with the bad inclination is, paradoxically, 'better.' For after having been wronged or injured, and turning toward another with hatred, I may, in a moment of calm reflection, come to my senses and experience regret. 'It was a bad moment; I had a bad day: the part of me that hates is not the part of me that I want to be.' Out of regret, repentance sometimes follows.

But I can also hate with my '*yetzer ha-tov*,' my good inclination, or with that part of my personality which I see as upright, and even moral. From such hatred, repentance rarely follows. For as I hate the other, I tell myself that I am justified in my hatred. The hatred in fact is my duty, a sign of my moral rectitude. And if anyone questions me, I try my hardest not to condescend to them as I explain to them, 'How could I do otherwise? How could anyone? Don't you know that it is a *mitzva* to hate?' 'We are obligated to hate evil.' I may even show you a verse in the Torah as I prove that hatred is my obligation. But devotion to hatred or the strident adherence to any position, Jonathan Lear writes, usually has another function: to keep me 'in the dark about who I am.' My unconscious, the part of me that feels ambivalent about my own choices and actions, causing me to lash out at others, acts through my so-called 'good inclination.'

This may explain why in our generation we do not fulfill the *mitzva* of hating evil in our fellows. Not just because it is hard to distinguish good from evil – as Milton wrote, 'good and evil grow up together almost inseparably' – but also because nowadays our 'good inclination' is suspect. The Hafetz Hayyim, one of the foremost sages of the last century, says, 'If you are looking around for *mitzvot* to perform – hatred is not among them – you will have to find another.' An earlier rabbi writes that the *mitzva* to hate evil in one's fellow applied only before the sin of the golden calf – before the trials and traumas suffered by the Jewish people. Since then, and certainly nowadays, the *mitzva* simply does not apply. For one who finds evil in another will likely find – upon examining his deeds – the same trait in himself. So not only is the hatred projected outward likely to be doing psychic work for me about which I am not fully aware, masking my ambivalence about myself, but it is a hatred from which I will never recover. I repent of what I acknowledge I did wrong, not what I consider to be a *mitzva*.

At the time of the Second Temple, the people of Israel were doing *hesed*, performing acts of kindness, with the wrong kind of 'good inclination.' They put a good face on things – the Temple service was flourishing, the Houses of Study were full, and the *hesed* organizations were thriving. But through these acts of kindness, their 'good inclination,' they showed what they were really about. '*We* are the genuinely God-fearing,' each group boasted. 'The way *they* serve God is not to my liking.' 'I don't like the *shul* where he prays'; and 'I don't care for how she dresses.' 'They may look like Jews, but they are not' – so each group claimed of the other. Kindness became a way of expressing exclusivity; *hesed*, paradoxically, the way to show hatred for others. Without the unity of the people of Israel, the Temple had, writes the Maharal, nothing to sustain its continued existence. So the Second Temple fell. The Jews may have been doing *mitzvot*, but they did not make themselves present to others. Just the opposite: the performance of the *mitzvot* – *hesed* as a form of hatred – allowed them to be absent to each other, because absent to themselves.

The sages say: 'Any one who has *da'at'* – or 'knowledge' – 'it is as if the Temple is rebuilt in his days.' Man is like the Temple in the way that he brings together different worlds. Betzalel, who constructed the sanctuary in the wilderness through his *da'at*, brings the divine presence or *Shekhina* down to earth. So the individual brings together upper and lower worlds through the form of knowledge the sages link to the human face: 'Just as every *da'at* is different, every face is different.' The individuality of a person is seen in his face; it is the place where soul and body, upper and lower worlds, come together. Shammai's injunction, 'Always show a good countenance, *panim yafot*,' or literally 'a beautiful face,' is not just a call for good manners. The beautiful face, the face that glows or shines, is like the Temple, called *hod* or beauty, where the physical yields to the spiritual, where God's presence rests. The Second Temple was built in the merit of Israel, in their making themselves present one to another. A person who has *da'at*, present to himself and present to others, participates in the Temple's rebuilding. He joins higher and lower worlds in himself.

When God's face is absent on the ninth of *Av*, it is not just a seeming absence. On other days, we feel joy, even intimations of redemption, but on the ninth of *Av* evil is palpably, irredeemably real. As the Psalmist writes, 'When You hide Your face, they are terrified.' And in the face of destruction and trauma, man's face is also absent. 'I could not see his face.' Absent in Auschwitz, absent in the traumas that make us unable to show ourselves or be seen.

Though the Temple was rebuilt, the Second Temple lacked, according to some of the sages, the divine presence; while others say the *Shekhina* was still present. True, the latter acknowledge, the divine presence emanating from Above was gone. But the Second Temple was built because of a different kind of divine presence, one with origins from below, from the people of Israel. Someone with *da'at*, who is able to join upper and lower worlds, who brings the *Shekhina* down to earth through his actions, is like one who builds the Temple. He makes himself present to himself and others. Though there is no immediate compensation for the sufferings of destruction, exile, and holocaust, there is the possibility of *tikkun* and repair – of bringing the *Shekhina* down to earth, letting it be seen in the human face.

Epilogue: Shmuel, Jerusalem, 2011

A beginning, by way of an ending: Shmuel was born eight years ago on the tenth of the Hebrew month of *Heshvan*, in October 2002. My wife woke me at 3 a.m.; we were at the hospital a half hour later. Not her first delivery, the labor was quick: by 5:45 she had given birth. As our son was transferred to the nursery, I was planning to make my regular 7 a.m. *minyan*. Our newborn would fit into my schedule, everything according to expectations; everything as planned. I accompanied the baby to the postdelivery room where the doctor, flanked by two nurses, labored over him, finally looking up to tell us: Shmuel has Down syndrome.

A close friend, a nurse at *Sha'arei Tzedek* Hospital – where more babies with Down syndrome are born than any place in the world – whispered an offer, 'I will take the baby and have him fostered.' The doctors agreed to let my wife go home after only one day, relieved that Shmuel would in fact be accompanying us. Friends visited: two conducted a dispute, in my presence, about whether a father of a child with Down syndrome should be wished a congratulatory '*mazal tov*!' (The answer, by the way, is yes). A rabbi in my neighborhood maintained, upon hearing the news, that Shmuel's birth was an expression of '*din*,' divine judgment; while someone else recounted that a father of a similar child proclaimed at his *brit* that the birth showed *rahamim*, divine mercy. A neighbor was more pragmatic: Shmuel was a blessing, but it would be best for the family – less of a burden for us, and less of an embarrassment for the other children – if we fostered him. Amidst all this, the languages of advice, explanation, and consolation – and I scarcely noticed at the time – there was an infant, nursing in my wife's arms.

The irony, unappreciated then, was that I had devoted so much time, read so many books, written so many articles about diversity and difference. I had been a fellow of the Israel Science Foundation, pursuing a research project on 'Pluralism in Literary Theory and Jewish Law.'

Plans for Shmuel, however, had not been on the fellowship application. Faced with a 'child of difference,' not the difference that may have been espoused enthusiastically around large oak tables by my teachers at Columbia and Oxford, was something for which I had not prepared.

When the world, as Deborah Kerdeman writes, 'departs from our expectations and desires,' refusing 'to be subjected to our categories,' we are 'pulled up short,' encountering a new world to which our old categories fail to do justice. I had been 'pulled up short' by the birth of Shmuel, a reaction, I found in retrospect disappointing. Not a trauma, though maybe experienced as such, Shmuel's birth marked the beginning of rethinking my attitude towards 'atypicality' and difference – and not only in relation to our new son.

The Biblical *tzelem Elokim* – man created 'in the image of God' – affirms the similarity between man and God, with all humanity created in His image. But as the sages explain, even in that similarity, there is difference: 'When a man mints coins with one stamp, all of the coins are similar to one other, but when the King of Kings mints each man from the "stamp" of Adam, the first man, each one of them is different.' Created from the stamp of the first man, and traceable to that original source, no man, however, is the same as another. But the image of God guarantees that all differences are linked back first to Adam, and through the first man, back to the divine. There are blessings recited upon seeing difference or exceptionality in God's Creation, but only the blessing over human exceptionality includes the divine name. Only in those human differences does the divine image dwell.

Multiculturalists may celebrate difference and pluralism, but not always when it is more than theoretical, when it really counts. As the *New York Times* recently noted, most prospective parents in the United States choose to terminate pregnancies rather than face the prospect of nurturing a difference that has a human face. Even the faces of those who *are* born sometimes remain unseen – in the past because they were hidden away, but now because we have trained ourselves not to see. Cognitive psychologists describe a phenomena called 'change blindness' – when a visual field, a painting let's say, changes ever so slightly, most of us will not notice the alteration. So the 'atypical child' does not register on our visual maps. Vision may be a biological mechanism, but what we see is also colored by perceptual habits and prejudices.

Bad advice is not always bad because malicious; more often, it is just unconsidered. We did decide to follow the advice of one of the celebrated midwifes at the hospital, in attendance at Shmuel's birth – 'Wait six months or so before telling the other children; let them come to love him first.' But an hour after returning from the hospital, with the children gathering around my wife's bedside, our oldest daughter, Elisheva, then thirteen, examined Shmuel for a few minutes, and then asked matter-of-factly: 'Does he have Down syndrome?' To which we assented with relief, happy not to have to continue the charade. With this, she disappeared from the house, and returned fifteen minutes later to pick up Shmuel and cover him with kisses. Our second oldest daughter, Avital, then eight, wanted to know: 'What is Down syndrome anyway?' After explaining to her what I understood about the syndrome, Avital, still unsatisfied, paused, considered and asked, 'Oh, do I have Down syndrome, too?' As parents we may try to model behavior for our children, but it was Elisheva and Avital who, approaching Shmuel's difference without judgment or prejudice, first gave me a model for seeing Shmuel.

About this time, I came upon a story recounted by the sages: Rabbi Elazar ben Shimon, returning from his teacher's house, was 'rejoicing greatly' and feeling 'proud,' having 'learned much Torah.' In his travels home, he 'chances upon a man,' who is described as 'exceedingly ugly.' When greeted by the 'ugly man,' Rabbi Elazar responded: 'Empty One! Are all the people of your city as ugly as you?' To which the man replies: 'I do not know, but go and tell the Craftsman who made me: "How ugly is that vessel that you made!"' The man may have been ugly, but he was also clever. Rabbi Elazar throws himself at the man's feet, and says, 'I have spoken out of turn to you; forgive me!' Only after entreated by the people of a nearby city does the 'ugly man' agree to forgive Rabbi Elazar, provided, the former stipulates, that 'Elazar does not make a habit of doing this.'

Rabbi Elazar's transgression had been perceptual. He was guilty of seeing according to habit, only looking at the outer shell of the man.

So the 'ugly man' invoked the Craftsman that made him: 'You may think I am ugly, Elazar, but despite appearances, I am connected to the One that made me, in His image.' In some readings of the story, the ugly man is Elijah the prophet, who comes to test Rabbi Elazar so that he does not become 'habituated to such behavior.' There are different kinds of bad habits, and some are of the visual variety. Rabbi Elazar's may have been learning Torah, but his 'pride' in his learning – the story's frame suggests – contributed to the failure of sight.

At the end of the story, Rabbi Elazar runs to the nearest House of Study and expounds: 'A person should always be soft like a reed and not hard like a cedar.' 'For this reason,' Rabbi Elazar explains, 'the reed merits to have quills drawn from it to write Torah scrolls, *tefillin* and *mezuzot.*' One should demonstrate the softness and flexibility of the reed. The Torah provides categories through which to understand the world, but those categories must be applied with sensitivity, and not 'arrogance.' When one is inflexible, like a cedar, the story suggests, it can allow for the perceptual transgression committed by Rabbi Elazar. Habitual ways of seeing – seeing through inflexible categories – lead to arrogance. Written as it may be with a reed, the Torah implies, through Rabbi Elazar's homily, that all of its categories, even those that come as the result of much study, are to be applied with flexibility and care.

So I had realized with Shmuel, and children like him. It is much easier not to see children who are different, through relegating them, with the simplifying glance of habit, to the categories of the 'atypical.' But even the phrase 'children like Shmuel' is probably a more expansive category than I had thought on the day of his birth. Since then, my family and I have been exposed to the exceptionality of difference, not just the theoretical ideal, but part of the everyday. Shmuel announces his difference with an exclamation point, so we have become the neighborhood bearers of secrets. Even the children who wear the badge of typicality, who seem to fulfill everyone's expectations, may have their secret – not failings – but differences. The boy who is always learning in the corner building has dyslexia; the 'Queen of the Class' has a learning disability. The revelations are offered with both sincerity and relief, their bearers happy with the consolation, 'we are not the only ones.' Yet, if we are fearful of revealing our imperfections or are reluctant to acknowledge the differences of others – I have found since then – it is not out of fidelity to the demands of Torah.

To the contrary, there is a way of seeing that is part of the inheritance of Jacob who 'leads on softly,' accommodating the pace and needs of his 'nursing' cattle and 'tender' children. Children with Down syndrome or other disabilities are not the only ones who are 'tender.' Seeing children – not just Shmuel, but any child – through categories risks missing the distinctive 'image of God' that each one of them, not just the diagnostically 'special,' represents. Sure, there is a continuum of exceptionality, but Shmuel, like almost all children, confounds categories; the most typical of children, if we take a close look will very often show themselves, in some way, to be atypical.

'Yet once more,' Milton begins one of the greatest of his poems. And yet once more: adjusting perceptual mechanisms – learning to see the 'tender' among us – is not a one-time affair. After a talk about my experiences with Shmuel, a distraught father in the audience of a newly born 'special' child asked: 'How are you so at peace with your Shmuel?' In explaining my 'transformation,' slipping perhaps into performance-mode, I may have mentioned the stories of Avital or Elisheva, or the image of Shmuel caressing his own younger brother in the hospital on the day of his birth, or Shmuel dancing with a *sefer Torah* on *Simhat Torah*. But, the next *Shabbos*, walking through our neighborhood, my wife and I passed a couple wheeling a large carriage to which was attached a very large respirator. The father, evincing special care, stopped several times to adjust it. '*Nebekh*,' I turned to my wife, 'how sad.' Her response was immediate, the rebuke barely camouflaged: 'But don't you see how much he loves his child?'

To the question, 'But don't you see?' very often, perhaps most often, the answer is: 'No.' Rabbi Elazar was chastened for a perceptual complacency born out of pride. I had been the same way with the father seeking advice and comfort. To his question, I should have answered that 'there is no magical transformation or defining epiphany,' but the ongoing challenge to be 'soft like a reed,' to be flexible in vision. For not just an ideal, difference has a face, through which the image of the Divine 'Craftsman' can be seen, if we only have the courage to look.

Citations

Unless otherwise noted, for the Hebrew Bible, I provide translations adopted from the King James Bible; for the Babylonian Talmud, I have consulted the Artscroll Schottenstein Edition. References to classical Jewish texts follow the standard editions and section divisions.

Prologue, Velvel

Sigmund Freud, 'The Uncanny,' *SE* 19.241; Exodus 31.3; Berakhot 55a; Ecclesiastes 8.1; Dr. Samuel Johnson, 'Life of Cowley,' *Lives of the Poets* 13; Genesis Rabba 9.12; Phillips, *Terrors and Experts* 84; Jonathan Lear, *Freud* 111; Berakhot 54a.

Part I Desire and self

'Making exceptions': Leviticus 19.18 and Rashi ad loc; Leviticus 19.34; William Shakespeare, *Hamlet* 1.1.1; Adam Phillips, *Of Flirtation* 50.
'Do it again, Denzel': Christopher Bollas, *Cracking Up* 205–210; Mishna Avot 4.21.
'Caught in the act': Eruvin 65b; Milner cited by Adam Phillips, *Beast in the Nursery* 63–7, 86–7; T.S. Eliot, 'Metaphysical Poets,' *Selected Essays*, 247; Christopher Bollas, *Being a Character* 75–81; *midrashim* cited in Joseph Soloveitchik, *Halakhic Man* 102–4; Isaiah 45.7; Amos 4.13; Mishna Avot 4.1 and Maharal, *Derekh Hayyim* ad loc; Gittin 43a; Shabbat 118b; Mishna Avot 4.18 and Bartenura and Maharal, *Derekh Hayyim* ad loc.
'Just dreamin'': Berakhot 55b; Genesis 41.12; Adam Phillips, *Terrors and Experts* 16; Jonathan Lear, *Love and Its Place in Nature* 207, 177–82; Genesis 41.8; Berakhot 56b; Isaiah 66.12, 31.5; Deuteronomy 23.5.
'The big game': John Milton, *Paradise Lost* 3.122, 7.591.
'Of rabbis and rotting meat': *Tana de-bei Eliyahu Rabba* 6; Leviticus 1.1; Sigmund Freud, 'The Antithetical Meaning of Primal Words,' *SE* 11.155–7;

Exodus 31.2–3; Berakhot 55a; Genesis 4.1; Maharal, *Netzah Yisrael* 1; Francis Bacon, *Philosophical Works* 268; Deuteronomy 4.39; Berakhot 58a; William Shakespeare, *Troilus and Cressida* 5.8.1.

'Identity is out!': Galatians 3.28; Norman Podhoretz, 'Scandal of the Particular'; Arthur Neslen, *Occupied Minds*, 280; Natan Sharansky, *Defending Identity* 47–75; Genesis 2.7 and Rashi ad loc; Joseph Soloveitchik, 'Majesty and Humility' 26–9; William Shakespeare, *As You Like It* 4.1.21–4.

'Isaac's bad rap': Maimonides, *Laws of Idolatry* 1.3, T.S. Eliot, 'What is a Classic?' 7–11; Genesis 26.18–19; T.S. Eliot, 'Tradition and the Individual Talent', *Selected Essays* 4; *Pirke de Rabbi Eliezer* 2–3; John Donne, 'The Anatomy of the World' 416; Psalms 81.10 and Samson Raphael Hirsch ad loc.

'Cheeseburger': Sifra 93d; Leviticus 20.26; Leviticus 19.2 and Rashi ad loc; Leviticus 18.3 and Rashi ad loc; Numbers 11.10 and Rashi ad loc.

'Writing an inspirational story': Sanhedrin 106b; *Sefer Yetzira* 1.1.

'*Eros* and translation': Yadayim 3.5; Song of Songs 1.2 and Rashi ad loc; Adam Nicolson, *God's Secretaries* 236; T.S. Eliot, 'Metaphysical Poets', *Selected Essays* 247; Song of Songs 4.5; Maimonides *Laws of Repentance* 10.5; Joseph Soloveitchik, *Out of the Whirlwind* 88; Psalms 34.9; Rashi, 'Introduction' to Commentary to Song of Songs.

'Swaying towards perfection': Adam Phillips, *Side Effects* 161–181; Mishna Avot 2.2 and Maharal, *Derekh Hayyim* ad loc; Vilna Gaon on Esther 10.3; Sanhedrin 106a, Numbers 25.1, Genesis 37.1–2, 47.27, 29; John Milton, *Areopagitica*, *Complete Poetry and Essential Prose* 955.

'Jacob's scar': Homer, *The Odyssey* 19.460–5, 510, 526, 536; William Shakespeare, *Romeo and Juliet* 2.2.44–5; Genesis 32.24–32; Hulin 91a; Samson Raphael Hirsch on Genesis 32.25, 33; Genesis 33.17; Genesis 25.27; Genesis 3.5; *Midrash Yalkut Reuveni* and *Shelah* to Genesis 25.25; Rashi to Genesis 25.25–6; Genesis 33.13.

'Torah and the pleasure principle': George Herbert, 'The Collar' 31–2; Freud, *The Future of an Illusion*, *SE* 21, 43; Robert S. Paul, *Moses and Civilization* 189; Joseph Campbell, *An Open Life* 24; D.W. Winnicott, *Maturational Processes* 140–52; *Midrash Tanhuma*, Ki Tisa 24; Megillat

Ta'anit 13b; Deuteronomy 1.5 and Rashi ad loc; Maharal, *Ner Mitzva* 2; Rabbenu Yona, *Sha'arie Teshuva* 2.12; Proverbs 15.30–1; Bava Kama 85b; Maharal, *Hiddushei Aggadot* 2.131; Plato, *Republic* 375; Mishna Avot 1.16; Exodus Rabba 29.4.

Part II Dispute and community

'Oedipus in a *Kippa'*: Sophocles, *Oedipus Rex* 14–15, 1070–8, 154–5; Jonathan Lear, *Open Minded* 33–55; William Shakespeare, *King Lear* 1.3.264; Hilary Putnam, *Reality with a Human Face* 170.

'Open minded Torah I': Mark Edmundson, *Death of Sigmund Freud*, 242; Bava Metzia 59b; Virgil, *Aenied* 4.346–96; Genesis Rabba 8.5; Eruvin 13b and Ritva ad loc; 'Introduction' to *Yam shel Shlomo*, Bava Kama; Ludwig Wittgenstein, *Philosophical Investigations*, 194; Numbers Rabba 13.15; Mishna Avot 3.11.

'Irony *Über Alles'*: Judith Warner, 'An Episcopal Passover': *New York Times*, 9 April 2009; Sigmund Freud, *Moses and Monotheism*, *SE* 23.207.

'Of false kabbalists and conjurers': D.W. Winnicott, *Maturational Processes* 145–6; and Phillips, *Winnicott* 141; Deuteronomy 18.10; Alain Finkelkraut, *Wisdom of Love* 72–73 Maimonides, *Guide for the Perplexed* 1.36; William Shakespeare, 'The Phoenix and the Turtle' 27.

'Modernity is hell': Thomas Hobbes, *Leviathan* 186; Numbers 16; Mishna Avot 5.17 and Maharal, *Derekh Hayyim* ad loc; Maharal, *Tiferet Yisrael* 18, Alasdair MacIntyre, *After Virtue* 8; *Sefer Hasidim* as cited in *Sefer Yosef Ometz* 88b; Maharal *Tiferet Yisrael* 18; Rashi on Numbers 16.1; Sanhedrin 110a.

'Lost and found': Makkot 10b and Maharsha ad loc.

'The poetry of the world': John Milton, *Paradise Lost* 11.319; Thomas Hobbes, *Leviathan* 81; Francis Bacon, *Philosophical Works* 474; Richard Dawkins, *River Out of Eden* 18–19; Ralph Cudworth, *True Intellectual System of the Universe* 136, 147; Ludwig Wittgenstein, *Culture and Value* 24e; Genesis 28.11; Genesis Rabba 68.10; Friedrich Nietzsche, *The Gay Science* 199; Maimonides, *Guide for the Perplexed* 1.8; *Pirke de Rabbi Eliezer* 4; Adam Phillips, *Of Flirtation* 55; William Shakespeare, *Hamlet* 1.5.166–7; Phillips, *Terrors and Experts* 84.

'Open minded Torah II': James Kugel, *How to Read the Bible* and website; Avram Montag, 'Communications' 90–1; Stephen Weinberg, *Dreams of A Final Theory* and 'Sokal's Hoax' 11; A.S. Eddington, *The Nature of the Physical World* 318; Louis de Broglie, *The Revolution in Physics* 18–19; John Searle, *The Construction of Social Reality* 175; Mishna Avot 5.17 and Maharal, *Derekh Hayyim* ad loc; Hilary Putnam, *Many Faces of Realism* 19; Bava Metzia 59b; Berakhot 58b; Makkot 10a; Eruvin 13b; Mishna Avot 1.14.

'Stepping up': Numbers 27.18; Jeremiah 1.5; *Mei Shiloah*, Pinhas; Exodus Rabba 33.5; Number 25.6–8; Psalms 106.30; John Milton, 'How Soon Hath Time' 1–4; T.S. Eliot, 'Shakespeare and the Stoicism of Seneca,' *Selected Essays* 110–11.

'Prayer and the people': John Milton, *Eikonoklastes, Complete Prose Works* 3.506; *Mishkan T'filah* and websites; Dr. Samuel Johnson, 'Life of Cowley,' *Lives of the Poets* 1.13; Psalms 130.1.

'A religion for adults?': Joseph Soloveitchik, *Reflections of the Rav* 96; Genesis 11.26–9 and Rashi ad loc; Joseph Soloveitchik, *Out of the Whirlwind* 152; Mishna Avot 2.1; Maimonides, *Laws of Temura* 4.13; Emmanuel Levinas, *Difficult Freedom* 11–23.

'Of fundamentalists, rabbis, and irony': Mark Edmundson, *Death of Sigmund Freud* 232–3; Jeffrey Perl, 'Civilian Scholarship' 4; Mishna Avot 5.17; Sigmund Freud, 'The Antithetical Meaning of Primal Words,' *SE* 11.155–7; Maharal, *Netzah Yisrael* 1; Jonathan Lear, *Therapeutic Action* 104, 177; Sigmund Freud, *Jokes and their Relation to the Unconscious*, *SE* 8.174.

'Don't take away my *mitzva*!': Proverbs 15.27; Beitza 16a and Rashi ad loc; Deuteronomy 15.8 and Rashi ad loc; Maimonides, *Guide for the Perplexed* 3.53; Joseph Soloveitchik, *Out of the Whirlwind* 209–14; Exodus 2.11; Exodus 3.4; Exodus Rabba 1.27; Psalms 89.14.

'Open minded Torah III': Stanley Cavell, *In Quest of the Ordinary* 172; Temura 15b–16a; Sigmund Freud, *Moses and Monotheism* 23.87–88, 135–6; Hilary Putnam, *Reality with a Human Face* 170; Adam Phillips, *On Flirtation* 21, 34; Jonathan Lear, *Happiness* 92, 102; Exodus 32.19; Shabbat 89a; Avoda Zara 5a; Eruvin 54a; Menahot 99a; Rashi to Hagiga 16a; William Shakespeare, *As You Like It* 4.1.4–5; Sigmund Freud,

'Recommendation on Analytic Technique,' *SE* 12.111–12 and Adam Phillips, *On Flirtation* 30.

Part III Time and memory

'*Carpe Diem*, Dude': Genesis 25.34; Genesis 15.7; midrash cited in *Beit Ha-Levi*, Toldot; Frank Kermode, *Sense of an Ending* 44–7; William Shakespeare, *King Lear* 1.3.264.

'The antidote for religion': Adam Phillips, *Side Effects* 50–54, Deuteronomy 18.13 and Rashi ad loc and Maharal, *Gur Aryeh* ad loc; John Milton, *Paradise Lost* 2.566–8; Psalm 27.10 and Rashi ad loc.

'Speech in exile': Genesis 2.7; Leviticus 23.24; Zohar, Exodus 3.9; Rosh Hashana 26a.

'Back to the future': John Milton, *Paradise Lost* 3.176–7, 207; Yoma 85b, 86b and Rashi ad loc; William Shakespeare, *Macbeth* 5.5.19; Joseph Soloveitchik, *Halakhic Man* 110–117; Kermode, *Sense of an Ending* 47; Maimonides, *Laws of Repentance* 1.1; Jonathan Lear, *Love and Its Place in Nature*, 158–68.

'Shades of faith': Deuteronomy 16.13; Exodus 23.16; Ecclesiastes 1.2, 3.2; Sanhedrin 96b; Maharal, *Netzah Yisrael* 35; Zechariah 16.14; Samson Rapheal Hirsch, *Collected Writings* 2.83–92; Deuteronomy 8.17.

'A special conversation': Jonathan Lear, *Freud* 140, 93–101; Exodus 20.8; Deuteronomy 5.12 and Maharal, *Gur Aryeh* ad loc; Sigmund Freud, 'Remembering and Repeating' *SE* 12.145–156; Zohar 1.32.

'Lighting up': Maimonides, *Laws of Hanuka* 4.12; Shabbat 21b and Rashi ad loc; Sota 49a; Megilla 9b; Genesis 1.2; Genesis Rabba 2.4; *Mishna B'rura* 670.6; Maharal, *Ner Mitzva* 2; *Tikkunei Zohar* 13; Number 27.20 and Rashi ad loc; Exodus 34.35; Maimonides, *Laws of Yom Kippur Service* 1.7.

'Whose letter is it anyway?': Esther 9.29, 31–2; Megilla 11a, 7a, 16b 19b; Aristotle *Poetics*, chapters 7, 9, 17; Exodus 15.2 and Rashi ad loc; Deuteronomy 31.18; Bruce Fink, *A Clinical Introduction to Lacanian Psychoanalysis* 52; Rabbi Shlomo Carlebach unpublished lecture; *Shulhan Arukh* 690.17; Esther 4.14.

'Cosmic consciousness': Exodus 10.2; *Sefat Emet* to Leviticus [5635]; Catherine Gallagher and Stephen Greenblatt, 'The Mouse Trap' in *Practicing New Historicism* 136–162; Maimonides, *Laws of Hametz and Matza* 7.6–7; Deuteronomy 15.15; Pesahim 116a; Genesis 2.7; Maharal, *Netivot Ha-Olam* 2, Path of Speech 2; Exodus 15.2 and Rashi ad loc; *Da'at Hakhma u-Mussar* 1.38.

'Trauma's legacy': Joseph Soloveitchik, *Out of the Whirlwind* 151–178; T.S. Eliot, 'Andrew Marvell,' *Selected Essays* 262; Deuteronomy 14.22, 26, 16.10, 13; Adam Phillips, *Promises, Promises* 257; Deuteronomy 8.17.

'Why I gave up biblical criticism': Solomon Schimmel, *The Tenacity of Unreasonable Beliefs*; Genesis 1.1 and Rashi ad loc; Deuteronomy 6.4–7; Berakhot 6b; Yitzhak Hutner, *Pahad Yizthak*, Shavuot 18.9; *Sifri, Va-ethanan* 8; Jonathan Lear, *Love and Its Place in Nature* 211; John Milton, *Paradise Lost* 5.538–40.

'Faceless': Exodus 25.8; Deuteronomy 31.18; Primo Levi, *Is This Man* 64; Maharal *Netzah Yisrael* 4; Esther 4.16; Mishna Avot 1.2; Yoma 9b; Leviticus 19.17 and Alsheikh ad loc, *Torat Moshe*; Deuteronomy 6.5 and Rashi ad loc; Jonathan Lear, *Freud* 211; John Milton, *Areopagitica, Complete Poetry and Essential Prose* 938; Hafetz Hayyim, *Ahavat Hesed*, appendix; *Meshekh Hokhma* 23.6; 'Introduction' to Genesis, *Emek Ha-Davar*; Berakhot 33a; Berakhot 58b; Psalms 104.29; Mishna Avot 1.16; Yoma 21b, Zevahim 118b.

Epilogue, Shmuel

Genesis 1.26; Deborah Kerdeman, 'Pulled Up Short'; Sanhedrin 37a; Rehamim Melamed-Cohen, *The Exceptional Child* 172–3; Amy Harmon, 'The Problems of an Almost-Perfect Genetic World,' *New York Times*, 20 November 2005; Ta'anit 20b and Tosefot ad loc; Genesis 33.13; John Milton, 'Lycidas' 1.

Select bibliography

Aristotle, *Poetics*. Trans. Gerald Else. Ann Arbor, 1970.

Bacon, Francis. *The Philosophical Works of Francis Bacon*. Ed. John M. Robertson. London, 1905.

Bollas, Christopher. *Cracking Up*. London, 1995.

_____. *On Being a Character*. London, 1993.

Campbell, Joseph. *An Open Life*. New York, 1998.

Cavell, Stanley. *In the Quest of the Ordinary*. Chicago, 1988.

Cudworth, Ralph. *True Intellectual System of the Universe*. London, 1678.

Dawkins, Richard. *River out of Eden*. New York, 1995

De Broglie, Louis. *The Revolution in Physics*. New York, 1953.

Donne, John. *Poetical Works*. Ed. Herbert Grierson. London, 1968.

Eddington, A.S. *The Nature of the Physical World*. New York, 1929.

Edmundson, Mark. *The Death of Sigmund Freud*. London, 2008.

Eliot, T.S. *Selected Essays*. New York, 1950.

_____. *What is a Classic*. London, 1950.

Fink, Bruce. *A Clinical Introduction to Lacanian Psychoanalysis*. Cambridge, MA: 1999.

Finkelkraut, Alain. *The Wisdom of Love*. Nebraska, 1997.

Freud, Sigmund. *Standard Edition of the Complete Works of Sigmund Freud*. London, 1974.

Gallagher, Catherine, and Stephen Greenblatt. *Practicing New Historicism*. Chicago, 2001.

Herbert. George. *Works of George Herbert*. Ed. F.E. Hutchinson. Oxford, 1941.

Hirsch, Ammiel and Yaakov Yosef Reinman. *One People, Two Worlds*. New York, 2002.

Hirsch, Samson Raphael. *Collected Writings of Rabbi Samson Raphael Hirsch*. New York, 1997.

_____. *Hirsch Psalms*, New York, 1997.

Hobbes, Thomas. *Leviathan*. Ed. C.B. Macpherson. Harmondsworth, 1982.

Homer. The Odyssey. Trans. Robert Fagels. New York, 1997.

Johnson, Samuel. *Lives of the Poets*. London, 1896.

Kerdeman, Deborah. 'Pulled Up Short: Challenging Self-Understanding as a Focus of Teaching and Learning.' *Journal of Philosophy of Education* 37 (2003): 293–308.

Kermode, Frank. *The Sense of an Ending*. London, 1968.

Kugel, James. *How to Read the Bible*. New York, 2008.

_____. 'Kugel in JQR.' http://www.jameskugel.com/kugel-jqr.pdf

Lear, Jonathan. *Freud*. London, 2005.

_____. *Happiness, Death, and the Remainder of Life*. Cambridge, MA, 2000.

_____. *Love and Its Place in Nature*. New Haven, 1998.

_____. *Therapeutic Action*. Pittsfield, NH, 2005.

Levi, Primo. *If this is a Man*. New York, 1991.

Levinas, Emmanuel. *Difficult Freedom*. Baltimore, 1997.

MacIntyre, Alasdair. *After Virtue*. South Bend, IN, 2004.

Melamed-Cohen, Rahamim. *The Exceptional Child and Special Education According to Jewish Sources*. Jerusalem, 2002.

Milton, John. *Complete Poetry and Essential Prose*. Eds. William Kerrigan, John Rumrich and Stephen M. Fallon. New York, 2007.

_____. *Complete Prose Works of John Milton*, ed. Don M. Wolfe. New Haven, 1974.

Mishkan T'filah: A Reform Siddur. Ed. Elyse Frishman. New York, 2006 and http://urj.org/worship/mishkan/

Montag, Avram. 'Communications.' *Tradition* 31.4 (1997): 90–91

Neslen, Arthur. *Occupied Minds*. London, 2002.

Nicolson, Adam. *God's Secretaries*. London, 2005.

Nietzsche, Friedrich. *The Gay Science*. Ed. Bernard Williams. Cambridge, 2001.

Paul, Robert S. *Moses and Civilization*. New Haven, 1996.

Perl, Jeffery M. 'Civilian Scholarship.' *Common Knowledge* 8.1 (2002): 1–6.

Phillips, Adam. *The Beast in the Nursery*. London, 1999.

_____. *On Flirtation*. London, 1996.

_____. Promises, Promises. London, 2000.

_____. *Side Effects*. London, 2007.

_____. *Terrors and Experts*. London, 1997.

_____. *Winnicott*. London, 1988.

Plato, Republic. *Republic*. Trans. Desmond Lee. Harmondsworth, 1987.

Podhoretz, Norman. 'The Scandal of Particularity.' *Commentary*: July/August, 2007.

Putnam, Hilary. *The Many Faces of Realism*. LaSalle, IL, 1987.

_____. 1990. *Reality with a Human Face*. Cambridge, MA, 1990.

Reflections of the Rav: Man of Faith in the Modern World. Volume 2. Ed. Abraham Besdin. New York, 1979.

Schimmel, Solomon. *The Tenacity of Unreasonable Beliefs*. Oxford, 2008.

Searle, John. *The Construction of Social Reality*. New York, 1995.

Shakespeare, William. *The Riverside Shakespeare*. Boston, 1974.

Shir Ha-Shirim, Song of Songs. Ed. Meir Zlotowitz. New York, 1977.

Soloveitchik, Joseph. *Halakhic Man*. Philadelphia, 1983.

_____. Majesty and Humility. *Tradition* 17:2 (1978): 25–37.

_____. *Out of the Whirlwind*. Eds. David Shatz, Joel B. Wolowelsky and Reuven Ziegler. New York, 2003.

Sophocles. *Oedipus the King*. Trans. Robert Fagels. New York, 1979.

Virgil. *The Aeneid of Virgil*. Trans. Allen Mandelbaum. New York, 1971.

Winnicott, D.W. *The Maturational Processes and the Facilitating Environment*. London, 1965.

Weinberg, Stephen. *Dreams of a Final Theory*. New York, 1992.

_____. 'Sokal's Hoax,' *The New York Review of Books*: 43:13 (August 8, 1996): 11–15.

Wittgenstein, Ludwig. *Culture and Value*. Oxford, 1980.

_____. *Philosophical Investigations*. Oxford, 1953.

Index